INSIGHT ⊙ GUIDES

CANCÚN & COZUMEL

POCKET GUIDE

◎ Walking Eye App

YOUR FREE EBOOK AVAILABLE THROUGH THE WALKING EYE APP

Your guide now includes a free eBook to your chosen destination,
for the same great price as before. Simply download the Walking Eye
App from the App Store or Google Play to access your free eBook.

HOW THE WALKING EYE APP WORKS

Through the Walking Eye App, you can purchase a range of eBooks and destination
content. However, when you buy this book, you can download the corresponding
eBook for free. Just see below in the grey panel where to find your free content and
then scan the QR code at the bottom of this page.

Destinations: Download essential destination
content featuring recommended sights and
attractions, restaurants, hotels and an A–Z of
practical information, all available for purchase.

Ships: Interested in ship reviews? Find independent reviews of river and ocean ships in this
section, all available for purchase.

eBooks: You can download your free accom-
panying digital version of this guide here. You
will also find a whole range of other eBooks,
all available for purchase.

Free access to travel-related blog articles
about different destinations, updated on a
daily basis.

HOW THE EBOOKS WORK

The eBooks are provided in EPUB file format. Please note that you will need an eBook reader installed on your device to open the file. Many devices come with this as standard, but you may still need to install one manually from Google Play.

The eBook content is identical to the content in the printed guide.

HOW TO DOWNLOAD THE WALKING EYE APP

1. Download the Walking Eye App from the App Store or Google Play.
2. Open the app and select the scanning function from the main menu.
3. Scan the QR code on this page – you will then be asked a security question to verify ownership of the book.
4. Once this has been verified, you will see your eBook in the purchased ebook section, where you will be able to download it.

Other destination apps and eBooks are available for purchase separately or are free with the purchase of the Insight Guide book.

TOP 10 ATTRACTIONS

TULUM
Perched on a cliff overlooking the Caribbean, it's the most beautifully situated of all the Maya sites. See page 50.

MÉRIDA
Full of colonial treasures and has a vibrant cultural scene. See page 64.

COZUMEL
Some of the best diving in the world is found among its coral reefs. See page 38.

UXMAL
Maya builders excelled themselves in its creation. See page 73.

ISLA MUJERES
The many attractions include snorkeling and diving tours, and spending the day on the glorious Playa Norte beach. See page 34.

CANCÚN
Days are best spent relaxing on the beach. See page 27.

PLAYA DEL CARMEN
With its great beaches and cosmopolitan atmosphere, this is the top tourist town on the Riviera Maya. See page 46.

MUSEO SUBACUÁTICO DE ARTE
Underwater museum featuring 500 huge sculptures in the waters surrounding Cancún. See page 32.

XCARET
An ecopark par excellence, has everything from an underground river to Maya ball games. See page 47.

CHICHÉN ITZÁ
The great Maya city has as its focal point the magnificent Kukulcán Pyramid. See page 55.

A PERFECT TOUR OF

Day 1

Beach attractions

Have breakfast at your hotel and head straight for one of Cancún's beaches – Playa Tortuga, Playa Chaac Mool or Playa Delfines. In the afternoon take a stroll down Boulevard Kukulcán, shopping for souvenirs and people-watching before finally settling down for dinner at one of the many popular restaurants.

Day 2

Water sports

If you're into water sports, the best place to go is Aquaworld in Cancún's Hotel Zone which has all kinds of water-based activities. Spend the whole day in the lagoon; snorkeling, observing marine life from a mini-submarine or enjoying a Jungle Tour. Aquaworld also arranges visits to an unusual underwater museum which boasts some 500 monumental sculptures.

Day 3

Museo Maya

Make it a Mayan day and visit the Museo Maya de Cancún. Take your time to admire exquisite Mayan sculptures, ceramics and jewelry and if you still have some energy, walk to the nearby San Miguelito and Ruinas del Rey archaeological sites.

Day 4

Isla Mujeres

In the morning take a short ferry ride to Isla Mujeres. There, visit Tortugranja to see endangered turtles and nearby Playa Lancheros to dine at one of the restaurants on the sandy beach. Then, at the southern tip of the island, head for the lovely Garrafón-Punta Sur National Park.

CANCÚN & COZUMEL

Xcaret

Rent a car for the rest of the week and drive south of Cancún to Xcaret, the largest eco-resort on the Riviera. You can take a snorkeling tour, swim in underground rivers or with the dolphins, and in the evening, watch a special Mayan show before finally returning to Cancún for the night.

Day 8

Uxmal

From Chichén Itzá drive to Uxmal to marvel at this jewel of Maya sites in the Yucatán Peninsula, with its splendid Pyramid of the Magician. In the evening enjoy a sound-and-light show and spend the night at the Lodge at Uxmal before driving back to Cancún the next day.

Cozumel

Take an early ferry from Playa del Carmen to Cozumel and spend the entire day exploring the island. In San Miguel, stop at the Museo de la Isla de Cozumel, then either go to the Chankanaab State Park to enjoy snorkeling or to the Parque Punta Sur Punta with its Celarain Lighthouse.

Day 7

Chichén Itzá

Begin the day very early and for several hours drive west to reach Chichén Itzá. Built between AD 800 and 900, the site has the magnificent Kukulcán Pyramid at its focal point and many more ancient structures to explore. At the end of this exciting day have dinner and spend the night at Hacienda Chichén, just behind the ruins.

CONTENTS

INTRODUCTION

In 1969, Cancún was a pristine, sandy island washed by the waves of the Caribbean Sea. But Mexico had begun to invest in tourism in the late 1960s, and the government was looking for a prime site to develop. Cancún was the perfect location for the world's finest multipurpose super-resort: The temperature rarely drops below 24°C (75°F) and it takes only a few hours to fly to the area from the US, Canada and other cities in Mexico. Work began in 1970, and today Cancún is one of the foremost tourist playgrounds. Its shiny, smart hotels with air-conditioning, room service and satellite TV cater to around four million visitors each year; its airport is the second busiest in Mexico. Natural beauty and wildlife can still be found, but they sit alongside thousands of people who migrate from the snowy, damp northern climes for a few days of R-and-R in this perfect environment. Almost everybody speaks English, and the US dollar can be used as easily as Mexico's currency, the peso.

WATER FEATURES

Cancún sits just off the northeastern coast of the Yucatán Peninsula, a finger of land bordering the southern rim of the Gulf of Mexico. It is a flat, limestone environment with little surface soil. This lack of soil means that little sediment leaches from the land into the surrounding seas, leaving the water crystal-clear, and either the deep blue of lapis lazuli or, around the shallows, a perfect aquamarine.

Though the landscape can be said to be a little monotonous, beneath the waves you'll find one of the most varied and active marine environments in the whole world. A coral reef, part of the Mesoamerican Reef (the second largest reef system in the world), runs south of Cancún, all along the Caribbean coast of Yucatán. The reef plays host to a permanent population of dozens of species of tropical fish darting fitfully around the polyps, and is regularly visited by numerous denizens of the deep, who use it as a pit-stop along their various migration routes.

Cozumel, farther offshore south of Cancún and once a pirate stronghold, sits on this reef, making it a natural attraction for divers and snorkelers. Its southern seaboard, made famous by diving pioneer Jacques Cousteau in his early marine films, is now protected under the auspices of the national park service.

THE LAND OF THE MAYA

In the Yucatán, the Maya reigned from around 1500 BC to the coming of the Spanish in the 16th century. The Maya have held a fascination for us since the first explorers found evidence of the sophistication of their society. Their calendar was more accurate than ours, they kept time, they were skilled in the use of medicine and surgical techniques, and they could build immense structures over 50m (165ft) high without the use of the wheel or pack animals. Yet when the Spanish came, the Maya were already in decline. Their knowledge seemed to have vanished with the

Tourists on the beach, Cancún

disappearance of a few of their highest caste. We still don't have all the answers to why the civilization declined as it did, and tragically, soon after the Spanish arrived, their priests – in the frenzy of the Inquisition – made huge bonfires of the precious Maya manuscripts. Their secrets, coded on the parchments, simply went up in flames.

The Spanish established their own towns in the Yucatán, often over the ruins of old Maya settlements; today pastel stucco walls, wrought-iron balconies, and geraniums in terracotta pots still give a feel of Castille, Leon or Madrid. Chief among them is Mérida, a beautiful city of shady plazas, handsome haciendas and horse-drawn calesas.

⊘ CENOTES

As far as geology is concerned, the really interesting features of the landscape lie beneath the surface. Acting like a giant sponge, with no surface drainage except along the southern border, the Yucatán is riddled with cave systems and sinkholes. Some of the caverns are dramatic, with superb stalactite and stalagmite formations. The sinkholes are the result of the roof of an underground cavern collapsing. Known locally as *cenotes* (corrupted from the Maya word *dzonot* by the Spanish), these are and always have been a major source of water for the local inhabitants; indeed the traditional settlement pattern was based on the existence of *cenotes*. In ancient times, the waters from the sinkholes were held to be sacred; at some *cenotes* within archaeological sites, vestiges of ancient pottery and human remains indicate that they may have been used for religious sacrificial rites. Today locals and visitors alike use them as swimming pools, as well as for diving and snorkeling.

Chichén Itzá – the diamond in an array of Maya gems – is only 2 hours from Cancún, and several other important cities are within traveling distance. While their ancient edifices are being rediscovered, the Maya people have been living in the countryside all along. Most are farmers, as their ancestors were, planting, harvesting and taking their goods to market. Their first language is often Maya – though of course

Cenote at Xel-Ha

Spanish is spoken by everyone except the elderly, and their faith is expressed through a modern Christian-Maya hybrid.

Some Maya have moved to Cancún, to make a living from tourism. They have been joined by thousands of others from all across Mexico who have settled here, spawning a worker's city on land that was barren only 40 years ago. Tourism has not only brought all the benefits of wealth but the problems of increased population, with its needs for resources and public services.

Cancún and Cozumel are made for pleasure, and no-one would blame you for simply sitting by the pool, basking in the sun. Yet to do that would be to miss the other facets of what the region has to offer: beautiful natural wilderness, the majesty of the Maya archaeological sites, picturesque Spanish colonial towns, and happy, welcoming people. Enjoy the hedonistic pleasure of resort life. But peek over your sunglasses occasionally. There's a lot worth exploring.

A BRIEF HISTORY

During the last 50 years, a great deal of research has been undertaken to discover more about the ancient societies of the Yucatán. Huge sections of their daily lives (and particularly the reason they came to abandon their cities) are still shrouded in mystery, but great strides have been made in deciphering their hieroglyphs and stelae (inscribed stone pillars). Despite these mysteries, there are few places in the world where the past feels as close as it does in the Yucatán. The thatched huts (na) that appear in 1,000-year-old carvings at Uxmal can be seen today in every roadside village. The stone *metates*, or grinding dishes, that grace many a kitchen, are identical to those left as offerings to the rain gods in centuries past. Away from the cities, the people still speak the Maya tongue, and their religious beliefs still bear the imprint of the ancient rituals of their ancestors.

☉ THE MAYA CALENDARS

Over the centuries, the Maya developed two different but interrelated calendar systems. The Maya Round Calendar consisted of 20 named days that interlocked like a cogwheel with the numbers one to 13, giving a total cycle of 260 days. Alongside this system was one more closely based on the sun's movement, with 18 months each 20 days long and a further five days at the end to complete the solar cycle of 365 days. These two calendar systems came back to their starting point every 18,980 days, or 52 years, signifying a rebirth. Interestingly, every 52 years was the frequency with which the Maya added a new layer to their temple-pyramids.

THE MAYA

The Maya's ancestors arrived in Central America many thousands of years ago. Small bands of Asiatic hunters migrated across the Bering Strait land bridge before 12,000 BC and gradually spread southward through the Americas. During the Archaic period (after 5,200 BC), these people settled in what is now modern Mexico. They developed a primitive agriculture, domesticating cattle and

Mayan ceramic figurine

cultivating corn, beans, chili peppers and squash (a pumpkin-like vegetable) in burned clearings in the jungle. Over time, a society developed that was so successful they could devote time to activities other than simple food cultivation. These people, known as the Olmec, are considered to be the first Mesoamerican culture, the one from which all others evolved. They developed a calendar based on a 52-year cycle, and also constructed pyramids for worship.

By 1500 BC the group that came to be known as the Maya settled in an area that stretched from the Pacific coast to the southern Yucatán, taking in modern-day Guatemala, Belize, the western parts of El Salvador and Honduras, and the Mexican state of Campeche. In the succeeding centuries they migrated into the northern Yucatán – an area that now forms the modern Mexican states of Yucatán, Quintana Roo and the northern part of Campeche.

Though their antecedents are still shadowy, they were much influenced by the Olmec. They developed and refined the Olmec calendar and counting system, and improved their building practices. The whole Yucatán Peninsula witnessed the flowering of classic Maya civilization and a society of great sophistication; with its magnificent pyramids, temples and palaces decorated with wall paintings and carved low-reliefs, a written language of hieroglyphics, and complicated medical procedures to heal the injured or the sick. Maya astronomers tracked the movements of the heavenly bodies; predicting eclipses and marking the times for the planting of the new corn. In fact, corn came to symbolize life for the Maya – in their myths of creation, mankind was formed from lumps of maize dough. Elaborate rituals grew up around the preparation of the *milpas* (cornfields) and the planting and harvesting of the crop whose success depended on the coming of the annual rains. These rituals were undertaken by a small number of initiates who controlled the knowledge of the Maya. Because the region has no surface rivers, rain was a precious resource and the Maya saw any stock of water, such as the limestone water holes, or *cenotes,* as holy places. The rain god Chaac was a very important deity, whose image can be seen at every Maya site.

Many colorful stories are told of ritual sacrifice practiced by the ancient Maya, although modern studies of their civilization largely dismiss this notion. Early Spanish reports describe how the natives threw virgins into *cenotes* to appease the rain god, Chaac. And you may hear tales of how priests marched hundreds of captives up a pyramid to cut out their hearts on the bloody *chac mool*, or red jaguar altar. Yet the Spaniards who arrived in Yucatán never say they actually witnessed a sacrifice. The stories often confuse Maya religious practices with the barbaric Aztec rituals that confronted the *conquistadores* who arrived at the Aztec capital in central Mexico. The Sacred Cenote at Chichén Itzá has been dredged twice and found to contain mostly jewelry, pottery and other artifacts. The few bones recovered are believed to be victims of the Caste War or of an accidental fall.

Maya civilization in the northern Yucatán reached its peak around AD 900–1200, but for reasons largely unknown – perhaps civil war, drought or disease – some of the cities were abandoned. When the Spaniards arrived, Chichén Itzá was crumbling but still being attended as a religious center, and the city of T'Hó, now called Mérida, was still inhabited by the Maya. The Mayapan and Campechan Maya in particular still had ruling and priestly classes who initially fought the Spaniards but who were eventually beaten in battle and co-opted into submission.

Reconstruction of wall painting of the Temple of the Jaguars at Chichén Itzá

IN THE WAKE OF CORTÉS

The first recorded Europeans to arrive in the Yucatán, in 1511, were doubly unfortunate: a group of Spanish sailors survived a shipwreck on the coast of what is now Quintana Roo, only to be sacrificed by the Maya natives. However, two of them were allowed to live as slaves and one, Gonzalo Guerrero, went native and married the chief's daughter. His children were the first *mestizos* – the people of mixed Indian and Spanish blood who now make up the majority of the Mexican population.

In 1517, an expedition led by Francisco Hernandez de Cordobá landed on the west coast of the Yucatán, near Campeche, but was beaten back by a hail of arrows from the hostile natives. However, the following year ambitious young Captain Juan de Grijalva discovered the island of Cozumel and skirted the coast of the peninsula, hearing tales from the Indians of the great civilization of the Aztecs. Here, they told him, you can find a city made of gold.

Grijalva's stories focused Spanish attention on central Mexico, and in 1519 Hernan Cortés landed in Veracruz, to

⊙ HOW YUCATÁN GOT ITS NAME

One story claims that the captain of one of the first Spanish ships to reach the peninsula went ashore and was met by a delegation of Indians. The captain asked the chief (in Spanish of course) 'What land is this?' and the Indian's answer was '*Ci u than*,' which meant 'I do not understand your words' in the native language. The captain heard this as '*Yucatán*,' and so the name stuck. Another theory says that the name comes from the local Yucca plant, plus *tal* or *hale*, which means the heap of earth in which the plant grows.

embark on an expedition that would end in the conquest of Moctezuma and the Aztec Empire. Though he had begun his campaign without the King's authority, once news of the treasures captured by Cortés reached Madrid, a royal warrant was dispatched to legitimize the victory and create 'New Spain' – the latest Spanish colony. However, it was left to Don Francisco de Montejo, 'a gentleman of

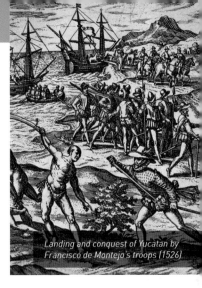

Landing and conquest of Yucatán by Francisco de Montejo's troops (1526)

Seville,' following in the great conquistador's wake, to take possession of the Yucatán in the name of the Spanish king.

Arriving on the coast in 1527, Montejo's forces were hindered by the dense jungle and withering climate, and were met by fierce resistance from the natives. To make matters worse, news of great riches discovered in Peru led many of his men to desert in search of greater rewards. The campaign went so badly that by 1535 the Spaniards had been completely driven out of the Yucatán.

In 1537 another force, under the command of Montejo el Mozo (the Younger), Don Francisco's son, set out to plant the Spanish standard on Yucatecan soil. At first ill fortune dogged them; the dwindling force was besieged in Champotón, on the west coast, for two miserable years. With reinforcements, the Spaniards managed to establish a beachhead. A band of only 57 men, led by Montejo el Mozo's cousin (yet another Don Francisco),

Act of faith

In July 1562, in the Yucatán village of Maní, Bishop Diego de Landa gathered together hundreds of 'idols' and all he could find of the Maya scriptures and in an *auto de fe* (act of faith) publicly burned them in front of the church of San Miguel Arcángel, thereby destroying virtually all Maya recorded history in a single night.

marched inland to take the Maya village of T'Hó. The Indians gathered their forces for one last great battle, and thousands of them fell upon the Spanish camp, now defended by 200 men. The horses and superior weaponry of the Spaniards gave them the edge, and they slaughtered hundreds of Indian warriors. After the battle, local chiefs made peace with the invaders and, on 6 January 1542, the Montejos founded the Spanish city of Mérida on the site.

THE CASTE WAR

Under Spanish rule, land was taken from the Maya and turned over to tobacco and sugarcane plantations, and the once-proud Indians were reduced to farm laborers. Franciscan friars, such as the 16th-century Bishop Diego de Landa, were dispatched from Europe to spread the Christian faith throughout the peninsula, though they met with some resistance – any similarity between the early Yucatecan churches and military fortresses is not accidental. Eventually, the Maya accepted the new faith, but combined it with elements of their old beliefs. Unfortunately, the Spanish were overzealous, and many chronicles relating to Maya beliefs and culture were destroyed (see box).

In 1821, Mexico declared its independence from Spain. Tension had been simmering for decades, fostered by Spain's treatment of her New-Spanish-born colonists, or *criollos* (deemed to be second-class citizens compared to those born in the homeland). Her trade laws decreed that everything produced in New Spain must first cross the Atlantic to Spain before being traded with a third country so that the proper taxes and tariffs could be collected. The geography of the northern Yucatán region separated it physically from the rest of New Spain, and fewer colonial landowners settled here than the area around the new capital (now Mexico City). Furthermore, this isolation led to the development of a strong independent streak for both colonists and indigenous peoples. The Yucatán declared its independence in 1821 but did not join the fledgling country of Mexico until 1823. In 1840, it changed its mind, and withdrew from the union. This was the catalyst for the Maya to take up arms against their colonial oppressors.

In 1847, a savage uprising known as the Caste War saw Maya rebels massacre white settlers and take control of nearly two-thirds of the peninsula. By 1850 they had driven the Mexicans back to their strongholds in Mérida and Campeche. However, in an amazing turnaround, the Maya's ancient beliefs became their undoing. Just when the Mexicans were on the point of surrender, the rains came early and the Indians, obedient to their gods, dropped their

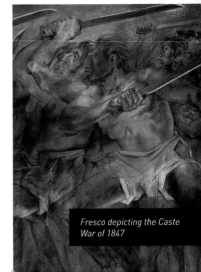

Fresco depicting the Caste War of 1847

Henequen farmer

weapons and returned to their *milpas* to plant the sacred corn. The settlers called in reinforcements and wreaked a terrible revenge on the natives. One group of rebels, known as the *Cruzob*, held out in the jungles of Quintana Roo around the city of Tulum, harrying the Mexicans and making the east coast of the Yucatán a dangerous area, off-limits until well into the 20th century.

THE HENEQUEN BOOM

Life was hard in the northern Yucatán, as the lack of surface water and the limestone sub-surface made it difficult to grow commercial crops or raise cattle. However, in the late 19th century, the hacienda, or plantation owners found a crop that grew successfully and was much in demand around the world–the henequen plant. The fibers produced by henequen could be made into rope and twine, indispensable for seafaring and international trade. Yucatán was the principal producer; exporting their goods through the port of Sisal on the northern coast. Processed henequen soon became known around the world as sisal.

The money earned by the plantation owners was spent on grand mansions along Mérida's Paseo de Montejo; they were filled with the best in furniture, porcelain and artwork. The Indians, however, worked the land for a pittance. In the east, some scraped out a living by tapping the sap of the zapote or chicle tree and selling it to American manufacturers of chewing gum. Unfortunately, when the henequen bubble burst in the 1930s with the advent of synthetic fibers, the peninsula fell into an economic decline from which there seemed to be little hope of respite.

Meanwhile, under the presidency of Porfirio Diaz, Quintana Roo on the Yucatán peninsula's eastern coast – named after Andreas Quintana Roo, a writer and independence movement leader between 1810 and 1821– was declared a territory of Mexico in 1902. Government troops clamped down on rebellious Indians, who continued to resist until a peace treaty was finally negotiated in 1935. The overthrow of Porfirio Diaz in 1917 led to reform and a new constitution, including a bill of rights for Mexican workers. At the instigation of local socialist leader Felipe Carillo Puerto (assassinated in 1924), many haciendas were broken up and returned to the people. But the Yucatán remained a backwater, largely forgotten and ignored. No overland route existed from Mérida to the rest of Mexico until 1949, when the first railroad arrived. Before then, all commercial travel to and from the peninsula, was by sea.

MEXICO'S MEGA-RESORT

Despite its considerable oil reserves and mineral wealth, debt, booming population growth, and grinding poverty had crippled the economy of Mexico by the mid-1900s. In an effort to bring more hard currency into the country, the government decided to promote tourism. A 3-year study of various sites was conducted by a consortium of government and private interests, and the deserted island of Cancún won out: not only was it a beautiful spot, but its use would revive the flagging economy of the Yucatán and finally bring Quintana Roo into the fold. The territory was eventually granted statehood in 1974, the same year that Cancún opened to the public.

In 2005, Cancún and the Riviera Maya were hit by Hurricane Emily and just a few weeks later, Hurricane Wilma, which stalled over the area for more than 24 hours. While the smaller resort towns of Playa del Carmen, Tulum, Puerto Aventuras and others were functional within a month or two, Cancún and Cozumel were the hardest hit and took the longest to recover. Many hotel owners took the opportunity to rebuild newer and more modern hotels. The unique sand-dredging process that constituted the only solution to beach recovery in Cancún was ordered immediately by the Mexican government. The process was time consuming and expensive, but ultimately successful. Within six months, 90 percent of the Riviera Maya was receiving visitors as if nothing had happened. Generally, the Yucatán peninsula falls within the Atlantic hurricane season (June-November) so visitors should follow current information on the development of weather conditions.

A pressing issue for the Yucatán is balancing ecological needs with economic development. What was a deserted coastline four decades ago is now a bustling Riviera. Coral reefs are being damaged by careless divers; lagoons that once teemed with tropical fish are now being polluted by suntan lotion; the beaches where sea turtles once laid their eggs are being taken over by sunbeds and volleyball nets; and turtles that once cruised the coastal waters are now an endangered species. Conservation projects from Akumal to the Sian Ka'an Biosphere Reserve give hope for the future, but the battle between development and conservation is set to continue, especially as in recent years the Riviera Maya has been one of Mexico's fastest growing tourist destinations, with well over 6 million tourist arrivals registered in Cancún in 2016.

HISTORICAL LANDMARKS

c. 1500 BC The Maya settle in the Yucatán.

AD 300–900 The classic period of Maya civilization, during which its finest structures are erected across the region, including those at Uxmal, Cobá, and Chichén Itzá (Old Chichén).

1200–1500 Decline of the Maya civilization, cities abandoned and knowledge lost.

1511 Spanish sailors land in the Yucatán.

1519 Cortés lands on mainland Mexico, declaring it to be New Spain.

1542 The city of Mérida is founded by Spanish colonists.

1562 Maya manuscripts are assembled and burned at Maní.

1821 Mexico declares independence.

1840 Yucatán State declares itself independent of Mexico.

1848–1890s The Caste War

1850–1900 The planting of henequen results in a boom that brings wealth to Yucatán landowners.

1902 Quintana Roo becomes a territory of Mexico.

1917 Porfirio Diaz overthrown; a new Mexican constitution includes a Bill of Worker's Rights.

1923 First reconstruction work undertaken in Chichén Itzá.

1949 A railroad track provides the first overland route linking Mérida to Mexico City.

1974 Cancún resort opens to the public; Quintana Roo becomes a state of Mexico.

1997 A new cruise port is built across the coral reef along Cozumel's western shoreline.

2005 Hurricane Wilma wreaks havoc in the Yucatán.

2007 The Kukulcán Pyramid (El Castillo) at Chichén Itzá is voted one of the New Seven Wonders of the World.

2016 The Mexican National Public Security System calls Yucatán one of the safest states in Mexico.

2017 The fourth terminal of Cancún International Airport is scheduled to be completed.

Tulum beach

WHERE TO GO

When the Mexican government decided to improve its economy by developing its tourist industry, a totally new, tailor-made, high-class resort was the aim; the major decision was where its site should be. Many factors were taken into account before a short list of locations was entered into a computer. When the final results were correlated, Cancún was top of the list.

CANCÚN

This location had many natural attributes in its favor. Twenty-seven kilometers (17 miles) long and less than a kilometer wide, the island is shaped like the number seven, and separated from the Yucatán peninsula by only 10m (33ft) of water. Its eastern shoreline is one **long beach ❶** of fine white sand, which is washed by the translucent azure waters of the Caribbean. Between the island and the mainland is **Laguna Nichupté**, a huge seawater lagoon bounded by mangrove swamps that are havens to numerous species of wildlife.

Today a string of hotels has taken much of the beachfront real estate, with the balance given over to bars, nightclubs and shopping malls. On the lagoon side, water sports and eco-tours abound in the calmer shallow waters. Blue signs denote public beach access and there are no restrictions, so you can walk the island's full length without concerns about trespass. All in all, Cancún has everything needed for the perfect relaxing vacation.

Finding your way around the resort couldn't be simpler. There is only one main thoroughfare, **Kukulcán Boulevard**, running the full length of the island, and every hotel and attraction is only a few strides from it. The addresses of most

Aerial view of Cancún's Hotel Zone

hotels or restaurants will include their position on Kukulcán Boulevard in kilometers; the farther south, the bigger the number. This guide explores the island from north to south, giving the exact location of attractions in kilometers to make it easy for you to find what you need. You could rent a vehicle of some sort to travel back and forth to your hotel, but there is a very reliable and inexpensive bus service stopping regularly and usually directly outside the major hotels, at intervals along the route. The buses run from early morning to midnight.

HOTEL ZONE

Crossing from the mainland onto the island – into the area called the Hotel Zone – the lagoon with its rich mangrove forest is on the right. This part of Cancún has the calmest sea for swimming and snorkeling, lying as it does in the shelter of Isla Mujeres just offshore. At km 4.5, just before the causeway over to the island, you'll find the **Embarcadero Playa Linda**, where a number of boats depart for sunset cruises and trips to Isla Mujeres (see page 34). **Captain Hook**'s offers a small fleet of pirate ships; shipmates eat lobster dinners, compete in contests and watch a show while sailing the high seas.

At km 5 you will pass a huge Mexican flag which serves as a landmark and can be seen from most points on the island. It is only taken down in high winds. Just beyond the flag on the left is **Tortuga Pier**, hosting boating trips and the ferry terminal, plus access to **Playa Tortuga** beach. Kilometer 7 sees a right turn to the 18-hole **Pok-Ta-Pok** golf course, which is located on a large landmass that juts out into the lagoon.

Punta Cancún, the area around km 8.5, where the island bends south, forms the heart of the Hotel Zone, the focus for activity of all kinds. A number of shopping malls can be found here, including **Plaza Caracol**, **Coral Negro**, the Mexican artesian market where prices are generally lower than in the malls, and **Forum by the Sea**, with several popular restaurants and a cine-complex showing the latest Hollywood movies. Dominating the scene here is the **Centro de Convenciones** (Convention Center), which hosts musical and artistic exhibitions: check the program during your visit.

South of the Convention Center is the Hotel Zone craft market – designated the Flea Market on the sign outside. Prices for crafts and knickknacks in this warren of stands are negotiable, and generally lower than in the malls.

Kilometers 11 to 13 are home to some more shopping malls. On the lagoon side, the first is **Flamingo Plaza**; a bit farther south is **La Isla Shopping Village**; fashioned after a Venetian lagoon and featuring many US-based franchise stores. This development also has several restaurants, nightclubs, movie theaters and an Interactive Aquarium where visitors can have a close-up look at tropical fish, feed the sharks or swim with the dolphins. Next to La Isla Shopping Village, Plaza La Fiesta sells all kinds of Mexican handicrafts and souvenirs and houses a Mexican bazaar. **Plaza Kukulcán**, at km 13 on the ocean side, features a luxury-brand shopping area where, due to favorable Mexican tax laws, customers can buy world-class brands such as Rolex and Louis Vuitton at the lowest prices in Latin America.

At km 15.2, on the lagoon side, is **Aquaworld** (www.aqua world.com.mx; daily 7am–8pm) which sells and rents just about every piece of equipment you need to travel on, under, or above the water; it is also one of the largest accredited diving instruction centers in Mexico. Head out into the lagoon on one of the fleets of jet-skis or small power boats, sign up for a snorkeling tour, or if you'd like to see marine life but stay dry, ride the *Sub See Explorer*, a mini-submarine with viewing windows so you get just as good a view as those in wetsuits. If you still have the energy, Aquaworld also offers Skyrider, a two-seat para-chair that floats in the sky across the lagoon, and Jungle Tour, a tour through mangrove jungles that ends with snorkeling on coral reefs. You may also try the newest popular sport in Cancún, the jet-propelled flyboard.

At kilometer 16.5 is a fascinating recent addition to Cancún's museum

Travel by bus

Taxis are very expensive in Cancún, particularly for travel within the Hotel Zone. So the best and cheapest way of getting around is by bus. Regular buses travel between the Hotel Zone and downtown, and they cost just a few pesos a ride. They stop outside all the major shopping and recreation centers and the main hotels.

Maya stone panel, Museo Maya de Cancún

scene, the **Museo Maya de Cancún** (Cancún's Mayan Museum of Archaeology; Tue–Sun 9am–6pm). It boasts an imposing collection of over 3,500 Mayan artifacts including sculptures, ceramics and jewelry, but only around 400 pieces are on display at one time. There are two permanent exhibition halls – one covering the archaeology of Quintana Roo and the second devoted to Mayan culture as a whole. The modern museum, with hurricane-resistant reinforced glass, replaced the original archaeological museum of Cancún that was destroyed by hurricanes. It was designed by Mexican architect Alberto García Lascurain and inaugurated in 2012. The admission price includes access to the adjoining San Miguelito archaeological site.

Kilometer 18 is the location of the the **Ruinas del Rey** (King's Ruins; daily 8am–5pm; free on Sundays), a Mayan site set in low jungle, and bounded on the lagoon side by the greens of

Museo Subacuático de Arte

the Iberostar Cancún. The El Rey buildings are not large by Maya standards. The temples were built in line rather than in a cluster, with the largest in the middle. Lizards about half a meter (2ft) long call the walls home, basking in the sunshine but disappearing in a flash if you venture too close. Opposite the entrance to the ruins is access to the most southerly beach on the main strip, Playa Delphines.

Toward the very bottom of the island, at km 21, is **Punta Nizuc**. The land in this area is mostly mangrove swamp and a haven for wildlife, being remote from the tourist activity of the Hotel Zone. But when you reach km 25, you'll find the side-by-side parks of **Ventura Park** (www.venturapark.com; 10am–5.30pm) and **Dolphinaris** (www.dolphinaris.com). Ventura Park features waterslides for all ages and Dolphinaris calls itself a 'state of the art dolphinarium' with Swim with Dolphins and Trainer-For-A-Day programs.

The Cancún region also has one very unusual attraction; the **Museo Subacuático de Arte** MUSA (www.musamexico.org), an underwater museum created in 2009 in the waters surrounding Cancún, Isla Mujeres and Punta Nizuc, at a depth of 3 to 6 meters (10-20 feet). MUSA consists of over 500 monumental sculptures, most of them by English sculptor Jason deCaires Taylor. You can visit the museum in a glass-bottom boat, you can scuba dive or go snorkeling there or you can take the Aquaworld Jungle Tour. To arrange a visit, contact MUSA or Aquaworld (www.aquaworld.com.mx).

DOWNTOWN CANCÚN

The Cancún Hotel Zone needs a vast number of support workers both for hotel service and continued development. Most of them live in **El Centro**, the downtown part of Cancún on the mainland just a few kilometers away, an area that was developed concurrently with the Hotel Zone.

Downtown Cancún, built on a grid plan, is dominated by **Avenida Tulum**, which runs north–south through the town. Here you will find stores, restaurants, currency exchange offices and travel agents. **Avenida Cobá** leads from the Hotel Zone into town; most of the important buildings on Avenida Tulum can be found to the north of Cobá. Firstly, the City Tourism Office on the corner of Cobá and Náder. Heading north, at the **Ki-Huic** craft market, the oldest in Cancún, you'll find the same goods as in the Hotel Zone at slightly lower prices. Following are the police station and Ayuntamiento Benito Juárez, the city hall. The traffic circle at the top of this block (Tulum and Uxmal) has a distinctive sculpture as its centerpiece, featuring carvings depicting the eras of Mexico's history. Just beyond this to the west is the modern bus station,

Crafts market

A good spot to check out souvenirs is Mercado Veinteocho (Market 28), just off Avenida Yaxchilán and Sunyaxchen. This popular market is filled with crafts from all over Mexico, as well as a wide selection of fruit, vegetables and meat.

Aerial view of Isla Mujeres

where buses depart regularly for Mérida and points south along the Riviera Maya to Tulum.

A block west of Avenida Tulum is **Avenida Yaxchilán**, where you'll find the main post office. Between the two is Parque de las Palapas, a small park and open-air concert pavilion, where local families meet to talk, listen to live music and while the evenings away. On the streets around the park – each named after a flower – there are small hotels and restaurants, plus stands selling a variety of fresh juices or hot snacks.

Avenida Tulum leads out to the north, and then veers east to **Puerto Juárez**, the port for passenger ferries to Isla Mujeres. These depart every half hour during the daytime, with both locals and visitors aboard.

ISLA MUJERES

Isla Mujeres ❷ (Island of the Women) lies only 8km (5 miles) offshore from Cancún; the 20-minute ferry ride transports you from an ultra-modern atmosphere to a small-town island vacation environment. Several companies offer one-day sailing trips to Isla Mujeres, often including lunch and snorkeling; they depart from Playa Linda and Pier Tortugas in the Hotel Zone.

Isla Mujeres now has a population of around 12,000. In past centuries, however, it was the haunt of Caribbean pirates, being far from the clutches of colonial overlords in Havana, San Juan in Puerto Rico and Panama City, the nearest colonial outposts. The first European to arrive was Spanish explorer Francisco Hernández de Córdoba, who landed in 1517 and discovered a number of small temples built for the fertility goddess Ix-chel. It was he who named the island. Isla Mujeres is no more than 8km (5 miles) in length, less than a kilometer (1/2 mile) at its widest point and split by inland lakes and bays. One main road forms an ellipse, following the shape of the coastline.

Ferries depart from various places in Cancún and Puerto Juarez and most deposit you at the north of the island, on the main pier of the only town on Mujeres. Craft stores and bars crowd onto the sidewalks and paved streets. The place bustles, especially when the ferries arrive. As afternoon turns to evening and the day-trippers head back to Cancún, Isla Mujeres takes on a much quieter character. The island has many loyal fans who return year after year for its particular atmosphere.

ISLAND HIGHLIGHTS

A few minutes' walk north of town is **Playa Norte** ❸. With its shallow, sheltered waters and fine white sand, this is a real paradise beach; the best time to get there is early in the morning before the crowds arrive, when you can pick your spot under a coconut palm.

Heading south out of town you'll pass the Mexican naval base and a small commercial airstrip before traveling alongside **Laguna Makax** on the right. Sheltered from the Caribbean Sea by the island itself, it has for centuries been a safe harbor during storms and hurricanes. Pirate fleets stopped here, because passing naval vessels would not see their ships.

Situated on the far side of Laguna Mekax is **Tortugranja** (Turtle Farm; daily 9am–5pm), which has played an important role in protecting six species of the endangered marine creatures and trying to build their numbers. Every year, nest sites are protected and a number of eggs removed. The hatchlings are cared for until they are a year old, and then returned to the ocean. You can see the young turtles throughout the year, but the best time to visit the farm is during egg-laying season; from May through September.

Further south, near Playa Lancheros, are a

Playa Norte

number of restaurants on the sandy beach opposite the mainland. Playa Tiburon is a perennial favorite, where locals and visitors alike come to eat, drink and swim. It is here that you can get a delicious and reasonably priced lunch of local fish, freshly caught and cooked on a wood-fire grill. A few vendors sell handmade jewelry as well as various gifts made from local sea shells.

Cross of the Bay

A bronze cross, almost 12m (39ft) high, weighing 1 tonne, was mounted in the sea between the island and the mainland near the Manchones Reef in 1994. The Cross of the Bay is a tribute to the men and women who have lost their lives at sea. Thousands of divers participate in a 'mass dive' here on 17 August each year.

At the southern tip of the island is the **Garrafón-Punta Sur National Park**, encompassing a rocky headland that plunges down into the great Mesoamerican Reef. On the cliff top at Punta Sur, there is a park that includes a bar, restaurant, various shops, the original lighthouse and an outdoor sculpture garden that appeared after Hurricane Wilma. The sculptures have been created by artists from around the world in metal, and look sturdy enough to withstand any weather. Footpaths wind throughout the park and along the cliffs, passing by the ruins of a Maya temple dedicated to Ix-chel, the fertility goddess, and equipped with observation points that were used to make astronomical observations. Just to the north of Punta Sur, on the west side, is the **Garrafón Natural Reef Park ❹**, which has been developed to provide facilities for divers and snorkelers. The shallow waters above the reef here are particularly suited to novice snorkelers. There is also a zip line ride here that gives visitors the sensation of flying over the blue waters of the Caribbean.

COZUMEL

Cozumel was brought to the world's attention by Jacques Cousteau's diving films of the 1960s. With the second-longest coral reef in the world just off its western coastline, it soon became a haunt for all those who enjoyed the underwater world. Today, along with enjoying status as one of the premier dive islands in the world, it is also a duty-free cruise port, with shopping to match the best in the Caribbean.

However, Cozumel has a much longer history of human habitation. It was a Maya site of some importance, being the center of worship for the fertility goddess Ix-chel. Cozumel became a destination for Maya pilgrims from all over the Yucatán throughout the post-classic period (AD 900–1530). The Maya who lived here traded salt and honey all along the coast; Xcaret was their major port on the mainland.

The Spanish conducted the first Catholic Mass in Mexico here after their arrival in 1518, but they had little interest in the island. It remained almost uninhabited through the 18th century. But following the Caste War, several rebel families settled here to escape retribution by colonial landowners on the Yucatecan mainland. They eked out a simple living for decades until the invention of the scuba tank. And the rest, as they say, is history.

Cozumel has multiple personalities; it caters to divers who go to bed early and rise with the sun, yet it also has occasionally raucous nightlife for those who want to stay out and party. Those who know the island well refer to this phenomenon as the 'wet' side and the 'dry' side. Day-trippers who arrive on their huge cruise ships – or on daily ferries from Playa del Carmen – add an extra dimension; they want to see everything in a few hours, so the slow routine of island life speeds up considerably when they arrive.

Plaza Punta Langosta, San Miguel de Cozumel

SAN MIGUEL

There is only one major settlement on Cozumel, the capital, **San Miguel de Cozumel**; it's a bustling town chock-full of souvenir stores, duty-free emporiums, bars, and assorted cafés and restaurants. If you arrive on the island by ferry from the mainland, you'll be dropped off directly opposite the heart of the downtown area, **Plaza del Sol**, also called the *zócalo*. This large, tree-lined square is where everyone meets for coffee, or lunch at one of the cafés nearby. Several streets surrounding the square are traffic-free, and you can stroll at your leisure among the stores selling T-shirts, pottery, onyx and silver. The storeowners have a practiced line and can be pretty persuasive, so it pays to have a sense of humor – or a few words of Spanish so you can join in the banter.

The street running along the seafront is **Avenida Rafael Melgar**, also known as the Malecón, almost constantly busy with traffic. It is lined with numerous duty-free stores selling fragrances, designer clothing, and jewelry and gemstones. Above these are bars and restaurants that keep the street buzzing until the early hours of the morning. Stop in at the **Museo de la Isla de Cozumel** ❺ (Museum of the Island of Cozumel; www.cozumelparks.com; Mon–Sat 9am–4pm) on Avenida Melgar, which displays some interesting artifacts found on the island and salvaged from wrecks around its shores. The two main rooms on the first floor offer simple explanations about the geology of the Yucatán peninsula and the development of coral reefs offshore. The second-floor rooms tell the story of Cozumel's history, from ancient Maya carvings to conquistador helmets and swords. There is also a room dedicated to the families who settled in Cozumel in the 19th century – after the War of the Castes – and who have developed the island since that time.

North of town you will find the airport, with several flights daily to other parts of Mexico and a few cities in the US. Several of the older hotels are located along the road here, though the rocky shoreline has fewer beaches than in the south.

THE WEST COAST

South of San Miguel, you will find the major cruise port at **La Ceiba**, around 3km (2 miles) from town.

Easy access

Traveling around Cozumel couldn't be easier. The island is almost encircled by a coastal road, the Costera Sur, and running across the middle, between San Miguel and the east coast, is the Carretera Transversal. The only coastal parts of the island to which access is limited are the northwest and southern tips, both havens for birds and other wildlife. The best way of getting around is by rental car or moped, but it's also possible to take a taxi.

Several large cruise vessels dock each week, bringing a flurry of activity. There is a good beach at La Ceiba and a number of hotels, plus several dive outfits have bases here – you can book a class or rent equipment. Farther south, in the ocean offshore, the reef holds the attention of even the most experienced divers because of its variety of marine and coral life. Turtles, rays, sharks and many species of colorful tropical fish can be found here, many at a reasonable depth for novice divers – though the reef walls are better left to those with experience. Almost all the dives off of Cozumel are drift dives. The booking office for Atlantis Submarine is also here; this mini-submersible is ideal for non-divers, allowing a glimpse of the thriving underwater world without your having to get wet.

South of the cruise port, the road leads away from the urban development and out into the countryside. This part of the island has some of the best and most sheltered beaches. In recent years, a number of excellent resort hotels have been built on large plots of land; you will see their gated entrances as you drive by. Next to these are the more modest accommodations that for years have catered to dedicated divers.

Around 5km (3 miles) from town you will find the entrance to **Chankanaab State Park** ❻ which has a beach adventure

Protected reefs

More than 80 percent of Cozumel's reefs are now protected within the Cozumel Reefs National Park, which was created in 1996. There is a small daily charge for diving in the park.

park (www.cozumelparks.com; Mon–Sat 8am–4pm). This was one of the first sites on the island to offer organized reef snorkeling. Snorkeling is still extremely good offshore, though the lagoon site is now devoid of marine life and is used simply as a safe swimming area. Dolphin Discovery runs the Swim with the Dolphins program there and the admission price to the program includes entrance to the park. The park's activities include a sea lion show, a demonstration Mayan village, areas for snorkeling as well as restaurants, bars and a dive shop.

South from Chankanaab you can stop at a number of fine sandy beaches on the west coast, some of which are free and some which charge a small entrance fee. The major sites are **Playa San Francisco**, **Playa Sol**, **Mr Sancho's**, **Paradise Beach**, **Playa Palancar** and **Playa Nachi Cocom**. All the main beaches have public access and each has its own café-bar, water sports facilities and lockers for beachgoers. The water is a beautiful clear turquoise color; you will see small dive or snorkel boats bobbing offshore as you soak up the sun. These waters offer some of the best diving and snorkeling in the world. The variety of marine life living on and around the coral reef here is amazing, with many of the largest migratory fish species paying a visit at different times of the year.

South of Mr Sancho's is a dirt road marked by an arch printed with the words El Cedral that veers left from the main highway. The road is poor and it requires some patience to avoid the potholes, but it leads to **El Cedral**, from where it is possible to ride a horse to Maya ruins deep in the forest (take insect repellent if you intend to make the journey). It was at El Cedral that the first Catholic Mass was said in Mexico, on 6 May 1518. In May each year the settlement reenacts the event and also holds a fiesta with horseback riding, music and dancing.

The very southern tip of the island is a national park, protected from the development, which threatened its wild but fragile environment. The **Parque Punta Sur** ➐ (South Point Park; www.cozumelparks.com; Mon–Sat 9am–4pm) was opened in 1999. Access is not permitted by car, but the park provides electric bicycles, buggies and a colorful open-sided tour bus to give access to the interior. At the car park an information center provides details about the park and its flora and fauna. Within Punta Sur's 1,100 hectares (2,718 acres) are the coast, with its wild beaches and sand dunes, and the interior lagoons and mangrove swamps, with a population of crocodiles and bird species. You can explore Punta Celarain, the most southerly point of Cozumel and now part of the park, and **Punta Celarain Lighthouse**, once protector of shipping in the area, and now housing the **Museo de la Navegación**

Crocodiles zone, Punta Sur

(Navigation Museum). A series of dioramas in both Spanish and English explain navigation methods through the ages, including those of the Maya who lived in the region. Before you reach the entrance, the Rasta Bar and Restaurant provides a place to sit, eat, drink and watch the ocean from a beautiful sandy beach.

THE EAST COAST

From Punta Sur the main highway heads north up the east coast. The conditions here offer quite a contrast to the west, with the waves of the Caribbean lashing against limestone rocks and the low vegetation leaning inward, blown by the sea breezes. The whole area has a stark and wild beauty, reminiscent perhaps of the time when Cozumel was the haunt of pirates and renegades. The tidal surge is very strong here, so swimming and snorkeling are not advised. Other than a few farms, there is little development until you reach **Playa Morena**, with its bar and souvenir stand. Here the road makes a sharp left turn to cut across the heart of the island. If you wish to continue north from here (on foot, horseback, or four-wheel-drive vehicle), you will eventually reach the northern lighthouse at **Punta Molas**, having passed the Maya ruins of El Castillo Real along the way. Take the sensible precautions if you make this trip – drinking water, sun protection, insect repellent and an extra layer of clothing are all advisable.

ACROSS THE MIDDLE

The road leading back to San Miguel, called the **Carretera Transversal**, hosts a few souvenir stands where prices may be a little lower than in town – if you're prepared to barter. Six kilometers (4 miles) from Playa Morena is the entrance to

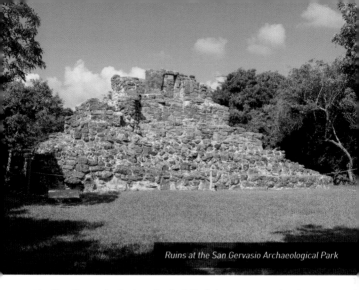
Ruins at the San Gervasio Archaeological Park

the **San Gervasio Archaeological Park** (www.cozumelparks.com; daily 8am–3.45pm). The remains of San Gervasio are located some distance from the site entrance, and though not on the scale of the major Maya settlements of the mainland, the beautiful tropical park environment makes the ruins worth exploring. Most structures date from the late post-classic period (1200–1530); the site was still in use when the Spanish arrived. At the **Estructura Manitas** (Little Hands Structure), you can clearly see the red handprints, dating from around 1000, on the inside wall of the temple. From here you can walk the route of a short sacred *sacbé* (Maya road) to the central group of small buildings. One is **El Osario** (Ossuary), where the remains of several Maya were found. Some 500m (1/3 mile) behind here is **Kana Nah** (Tall House), which is one of the largest structures at the site. It was the main temple, where the fertility goddess, Ix-chel, was worshipped.

ALONG THE RIVIERA MAYA TO TULUM

When tourism first came to this area of the Yucatán Peninsula, the coastline between Cancún and Tulum was a pristine natural landscape, broken only by a few villages. Rocky coastal inlets where seawater mingles with the freshwater of several *cenotes* were separated by acres of virgin mangrove. Parts of the coastline still have sandy beaches that seem as if no human has ever set foot on them.

Of course, with the success of Cancún, developers have looked for other opportunities in the region, and this stretch of coastline is gradually being taken over by tourist development. Luckily, not every development mimics the grand resorts of Cancún, and there is some variety here, in both style and atmosphere; there are a number of all-inclusive hotel complexes, yet there are also interesting towns and ports. Tulum, with its magnificent Maya ruins, forms a natural southerly point to the strip of coastal development, which has been given the name 'The Riviera Maya.' The area is easy to explore by vehicle, as Highway 307, the main road following the coastline – though in some places a few kilometers inland from it – is in good condition; most of it is now a four-lane highway. There is also an excellent bus service linking the major settlements and large hotels, which takes around 2 hours to run the whole length of the Riviera.

PLAYA DEL CARMEN

Traveling south from Cancún, the first town you will pass at 36km (22 miles) is **Puerto Morelos**, a growing expatriate beachside community and the port for vehicle ferries to Cozumel. Further south, **Playa del Carmen ❽**, once a tiny settlement, is now the fastest growing resort in the area, and

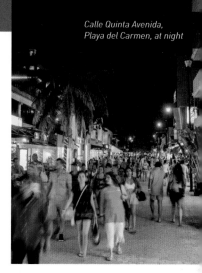

one of the fastest growing cities in the Americas. Once just a stepping-stone to Cozumel, Playa del Carmen is now a major international destination in its own right. A variety of hotels sit on a popular beach beside clear, bright azure water. Avenida 5, or Fifth Avenue, is the main shopping street which runs parallel to the beach and is closed during most of the day to car traffic.

XCARET

Beyond Playa the coastline is most dramatic; the limestone has been eroded into several coastal inlets, lagoons and riverbeds. This stretch is excellent for snorkeling and has some exciting *cenotes* for diving and swimming. In addition, a number of these inlets have been protected as national parks or developed as pleasure playgrounds for tourists.

Around 10km (6 miles) south of Playa del Carmen, **Xcaret** ❾ (www.xcaret.com, pronounced 'ish-car-ett'; daily 8.30am–10.30pm) is the largest eco-resort on the Riviera, and one which has won the most awards. Once the site of an ancient Maya port for departures to Cozumel, the sheltered Xcaret lagoons provided the perfect protection for canoes and were a common location for purification rituals. The remains of several temples dotted around the park add to the mystery and adventure of the Xcaret experience.

Snorkelers at Xcaret

When it opened in 1990, the focus was mainly on snorkeling in the cenotes and lagoon. Now activities like the Underground Rivers, the Aquatic Paradise and Dolphin Ride and the Snuba and SeaTrek programs have greatly expanded Xcaret's offerings. The grounds include beaches, a butterfly pavilion, a zoo, a bee farm, Jaguar Island, a coral reef aquarium, a mushroom farm, a bat cave and much more. Xcaret also has the largest and most effective loggerhead and green sea turtle protection and breeding program in Mexico. This program includes protecting breeding and nesting grounds, as well as educating both local schoolchildren and visitors about the turtles. Visitors to the park can see the turtles at different stages of their growth and development, from tiny babies to the very large full-grown turtles that are released back into the wild. Xcaret has special programs for the late afternoon and evening, including demonstrations of the Maya Ball Game in the replica ball court, re-enactments of ancient Maya rituals and musical 'spectaculars' in the main amphitheater.

PUERTO AVENTURAS AND XEL-HA

Puerto Aventuras is an interesting development, unlike any place else on the Maya Riviera. The rocky coastal inlets have been transformed into a magnificent marina, with mooring for yachts and motor launches and a walkway along the waterside. Two- and three-story buildings line the marina, with restaurants and shops at ground level, giving Puerto Aventuras the feel of the Italian or French Riviera. At the center of the resort, in the sheltered waters of the lagoon, there is a Dolphin Discovery program for swimming with the dolphins.

Just south of Puerto Aventuras is **Xel-Ha** ❿ (www.xelha. com; daily 8.30am–6.30pm), a network of mangroves, water-ways, pools and caves. It too offers a Swim with the Dolphin program, with a whole area called Dolphins World dedicated to educating and supporting the people taking part in the program.

North of Xel-Ha, the still-sleepy beach village of **Akumal** provides world-class diving and fishing opportunities. Hidden among the palm trees are a few of the coasts' best restaurants (Turtle Bay Café and Bakery) and bars (Buena Vida bar and restaurant), as well as a variety of small hotels and condos available for vacation rental. Akumal Dive Center and Akumal Dive Shop are among the area's oldest and most trusted PADI dive centers.

Puerto Aventuras

TULUM

There are three Tulums from which to choose: the Maya ruins, the small inland town and the beach community.

The Maya ruin of **Tulum** ⑪ (daily 8am–5pm) is the most dramatically situated ruin on the Yucatán Peninsula, perched on a cliff above the blue Caribbean sea. Buses and cars park near a handicraft market about 1/2 mile (800 meters) from the entrance. There is an open-sided shuttle bus if it's too hot to walk.

Tulum was built late in Maya history, during the 12th century and the settlement was still thriving when the Spaniards arrived. This was a time of upheaval, so the Maya built their temples surrounded by a strong defensive wall – the name 'Tulum' means 'walled' or 'fenced'. Maya lives were saved by those walls during the Caste War when several rebels brought their families to hide out there.

⊙ GUIDE TO THE MAYA GODS

The Maya worshiped a series of gods who they believed controlled their world. Each had its own sphere of responsibility that, when they worked together, provided full lives and good harvests. Here is a list of the most important:

Chaac: the god of rain, harvest, cenotes, lightning, tobacco and the cardinal points.

Itzamná: the supreme god of creation, who gave the Maya corn and written language.

Ix-chel: the goddess of women's fertility, medicine, childbirth, weaving and the moon.

Kinich Ahau: the sun god.

Kukulcán (called *Quetzalcóatl* by the Toltecs): half god/half mortal who taught the Maya how to cultivate and use cocoa.

There are no large structures on the scale of those in Chichén Itzá or Uxmal, but several sit on rocky outcrops overlooking the sandy beach and blue water, making them a photographer's delight. Tulum was dedicated to the worship of the Descending God, who can be seen in carvings and stucco reliefs on El Castillo, the main temple, and other buildings on the site.

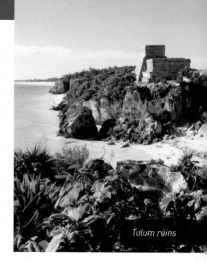
Tulum ruins

Tulum, the town or village along the main highway, is south of the ruins. Its sandy streets have been paved and the storefronts are filling quickly with restaurants and stores catering to a growing number of visitors. The town also has ATM machines, grocery stores, drug stores, and low-priced hostels and hotels. The road which goes straight through the center of town continues on to **Xcalak**, **Mahajual** and **Chetumal**.

The third Tulum can be found along the beach on the Boca Paila road, 1.5km (1 mile) east of town. This narrow paved road begins at the ruins and travels south along the shore all the way through the **Sian Ka'an Biosphere Reserve** (see page 71) to **Punta Allen**, a sleepy fishing village. The road is easy to travel up to the gate of the Reserve, but pot-holed and difficult farther south. It is lined on the beach side with hotels, bungalows, condos, restaurants and bars. These are all ecologically low-impact buildings, mostly with palapa roofs, where the electricity still turns off before midnight, allowing lucky visitors a dramatic view of the starry heavens. The beaches in Tulum are the same kind of white sandy expanses that are found in Cancún, but flanked by fewer and much smaller establishments.

COBÁ

Inland from Tulum is another Maya site worthy of note. **Cobá** ⑫ (daily 8am–5pm) sits surrounded by jungle some 42km (26 miles) from Tulum on the banks of Lake Cobá. It is one of the largest Maya sites, said by archaeologists to be 100 sq km (39 sq miles) in area, and encompasses around 20,000 separate structures – though most have not been excavated. It is thought that at its peak (AD 800–1000), it was one of the most important cities in the Maya world, with a network of roads

---

⊙ STEPHENS AND CATHERWOOD

When news of the Maya settlements of Guatemala and Belize first reached the outside world, two men – American diplomat John Lloyd Stephens and the English artist Frederick Catherwood – decided to travel to Yucatán to explore the region for more evidence. Their first expedition in 1841 almost ended in disaster, when Catherwood became ill with fever. However, the pair returned in 1843 and found the remains of many now-famous ancient sites, including Uxmal and Chichén Itzá.

Stephens wrote a fascinating account of the travels the pair undertook, illustrated by Catherwood's beautiful paintings. The works *Incidents of Travel in Central America, Chiapas, and Yucatán* and *Incidents of Travel in Yucatán* are still in print and would make a great accompaniment to your own explorations.

reaching to many satellite settlements, some up to 100km (60 miles) away.

Climbing Nohoch Mul

At Cobá it is possible to feel a little as Stephens and Catherwood must have done when they rediscovered the Maya sites in their expeditions of 1841. Most of the pyramids and temples still lie under centuries of debris and vegetation, tantalizing visitors with intricate carvings peeking through roots and branches. Here you can imagine yourself to be exploring where no one except the abundant birds and butterflies has been for centuries. Cobá – more than any other site in the area – requires sensible footwear, hat, sunscreen and bottled water, because the principal structures are spread so wide apart.

The main building at the site is the **Iglesia** or church, a huge pyramid nearly 30m (90ft) high. It sits among a number of structures known as the **Grupo Cobá**, which lie to the right of the main entrance. Its major staircase has been cleared, and the view from the top is spectacular, with the lakes and jungle stretching out to cover the land. At irregular intervals, vegetation-covered mounds indicate other pyramids yet to be freed.

The only other large structure in view is the stone facade of **Nohoch Mul** (Big Hill) some 20 minutes' walk away. At 42m (138ft), Nohoch Mul is one of the tallest Maya pyramids ever discovered; there are 120 steps to its upper platform. Once there you will find images of the Descending God – the same image seen so often at Tulum. Between the Nohoch Mul group and Grupo Cobá is **Conjunto de las Pinturas** (Paintings Group) where you can see the Pyramid of the Painted Lintel, which, as the name suggests, still bears traces of its original coloring.

CANCÚN TO MÉRIDA

Traveling west out of the Cancún region transports you almost immediately into a different era. Traces of Spanish colonial life dot the landscape, but more than this, once out in the country-side the life of the agricultural worker very much resembles that lived by Maya in centuries past. Today they still produce numerous crops on their small farms *(milpas)*.

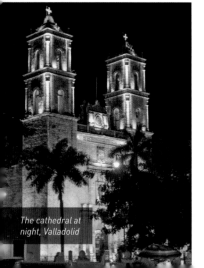

The cathedral at night, Valladolid

Two highways travel west: the four-lane toll highway carries traffic halfway across the Yuca-tán peninsula in around 3 hours; the local road trav-els through the countryside and many local settle-ments, giving an oppor-tunity to view the daily life of the region. Both roads are numbered 180, but the local road is signposted '180 libre' (meaning free) and involves numerous *topes* or speed bumps.

VALLADOLID

The first major town on the 180 libre is **Valladolid**. Founded in 1543, it has the Yucatán's oldest church, **San Bernardino de Siena** (1552), now outshone by the imposing **Catedral de San Gervasio** in the main square. North of Valladolid on route 295 are the remains of the Maya city of **Ek Balam ⑬** (daily 8am–5pm). The scale of the buildings and their excellent restoration make this one of the most impressive Maya sites in the Yucatán. The main structures are grouped around two connecting spaces called the Central and Southern Plazas, with the Ball Court in between. At the north end of the site is the enormous main pyramid, or 'Acropolis', all of 160m (525ft) wide and 31m (100ft) high. On its restored flank is one of the most elaborate decorative friezes ever discovered in the Maya world, representing Itzamná, the God of Creation.

Continuing east, just before Chichén Itzá are the **Grutas de Balancanché ⑭** (Balancanché Caves; daily 9am–5pm; guided tours in English at 11am, 1 and 3pm), which were only rediscovered in 1959 after being abandoned by the Maya. The huge caverns with underground lakes were a place of offering, and evidence of incense burning can still be found.

CHICHÉN ITZÁ

Three hours of traveling will bring you to the small town of **Pisté** and the remains of one of the most famous Maya sites. **Chichén Itzá ⑮** (daily 8am–5pm; Light and Sound show at 8pm in summer and 7pm in winter) has fired the imagination of archaeologists and tourists for many years, and in 2007 was designated one of the New Seven Wonders of the World. No matter how many other people happen to be there when you visit, the crowds are dwarfed by the size and grandeur of the well-excavated structures.

The original Maya city at Chichén Itzá (Old Chichén) was built late in the empire's cycle, between 800 and 900 (the terminal classic period). Despite large amount of research, historians are

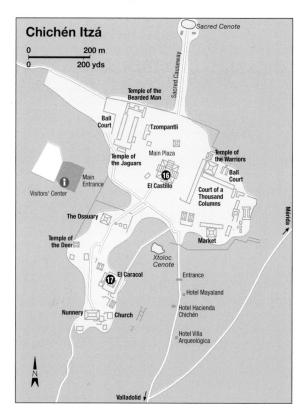

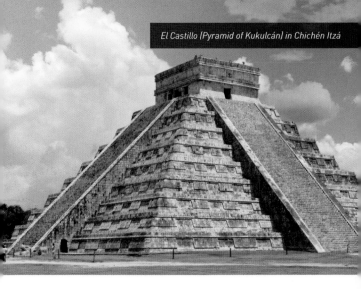

El Castillo (Pyramid of Kukulcán) in Chichén Itzá

still not in agreement as to exactly how the city evolved and what influences came to bear. What is certain is that Toltec influences, in the form of the god Quetzalcóatl (Kukulcán) and Chaac-Mool sculptures can be found here, along with traditional Maya symbols. Another mystery yet to be solved is why the Toltec abandoned the city in 1200. Some time later, in the 13th century, the Itzá, a Maya tribe led by a ruler named Itzámna, moved north out of what is now the Campeche province to the tip of Yucatán and settled in the city. They gave the city the name Chichén Itzá, which means 'Mouth of the Well of the Itzás', and founded a capital at Mayapan, near the site of the modern city of Mérida. In the 15th century, following a bloody civil war, the Itzás abandoned Chichén Itzá as a place to live, and by the time the Spanish set foot on the peninsula it was used only as a ceremonial center.

Chichén Itzá occupies 6 sq km (4 sq miles). If you want to explore all corners of the site, a visit will occupy a full day.

Excursions from Cancún are popular but can be tiring. It is far better to stay near the site (hotels adjacent to the site itself, in nearby Pisté and in Valladolid) and begin your visit early, because you can start when the day is cooler, and you will be able to see at least some of the site before the tour groups arrive. Those who stay overnight can also enjoy the sound-and-light show that takes place each evening. You can visit the site unaccompanied or hire a guide at the entrance, where there is a bookstore, jewelry store, restaurant, money exchange, ATM, cappuccino and hot dog stands, bathrooms and a model of the city to help you get your bearings.

The city has two distinct sectors. In Old Chichén, in the south end of the park, the structures are built in the Puuc-Maya style (see page 72) with arched stone roofs. The newer

Ik-Kil cenote

section has distinct Toltec influences, with stone columns supporting roofs constructed with wooden beams. This allowed rooms in New Chichén to be much larger than in the older part of the site, but it also meant that as the wood rotted, the roofs of the chambers collapsed, leaving these structures less intact today.

Refreshing swim

Ik-Kil *cenote*, just 2km (1 mile) before Chichén Itzá, is a great place for a cool swim. The *cenote* is open to the sky, with waterfalls and jungle creepers overhead. There is cabaña accommodation available, and a pleasant restaurant set in lush gardens.

As you enter the site (in the new part of the city) the huge square edifice of **El Castillo** ⑯, also called the Pyramid of Kukulcán, comes into view on your right. The pyramid, 30m (100ft) high and the main time-keeping mechanism of the city, was built very precisely in position, shape and height in order to predict the planting and harvesting cycles. There are 364 steps in four staircases, which together with the final step up to the summit platform represent the 365 days of the year. There are 52 panels on each side, which echo the 52-year cycle of the Maya calendar, and terraces that parallel the main staircase, representing the 18-month solar cycle. The best time to see this super-sized timepiece in action is at the Spring Equinox (March 21) or Fall Equinox (September 21) in the afternoon, when the sun's rays fall down the northern stairway and hit the serpent head at the base. With the play of light and shadow, the serpent appears to wriggle down into the earth. For the Maya, this signified the refertilization of the land – and time to plant the corn. The light then leaves the snake head first and travels back up from the base; the Maya believed that the power of the sun was returning to the realm of the gods in the sky.

To the left of the main entrance is the huge, open, main **Juego de Pelota** (ball court), one of the best preserved and largest in Central America. Although one of nine on the site, it is definitely the most impressive, with walls 8m (26ft) high, 83m (272ft) long, and set 30m (98ft) apart. The walls are decorated with friezes showing players dressed in protective clothing and a rather bloodthirsty victor with the head of a losing player (though some archaeologists believe that the victor had the 'honor' of losing his life at the end of the match). This ball court has been well studied by archaeologists; ball courts can be found in most Mesoamerican settlements, but the true purpose of the games is still not fully understood.

There are temples at each end of the court, which add to the superb acoustics: it is possible to hear a voice speaking at one end clearly at the other, and the whole complex has a seven-repeat echo, a sacred number in Maya society. The temple attached to the eastern wall, the **Templo de los Jaguares** (Temple of the Jaguars), is named in honor of the jaguar figures carved on the upper panels of the temple and a statue of a jaguar in the lower chamber. The carving to its left is said to depict the Maya creation myth.

Next to the ball courts is **Tzompantli**, Temple of the Skulls, with long rows of skulls carved into its main platform. It is said that here the victims of sacrifice had their heads impaled on poles for the edification of the gods. Beside this is the **Plataforma de las Águilas** (Platform of the Eagles), with reliefs of eagles and jaguars clutching human hearts. Equidistant between El Castillo and the Temple of the Skulls, the **Plataforma de Venus** was dedicated to the worship of the planet Venus, a common deity among the Maya, and has motifs around its side which are thought to show the head of the planet emerging from a monster-serpent.

From the platform, a sacred causeway called a sac'be (which means 'white road' in Maya) leads to one of the most important religious sites in the city, the natural feature which may have given the city its name. The **Cenote Sagrado**, a limestone water-hole, 60m (90 ft) in diameter and 21m (69 ft) from rim to water level, supplied fresh water to the city. It may also have served ritual religious purposes, as when it was dredged by Edward Thompson, the archaeologist, various statues and religious artifacts were found. Contrary to popular stories, scholars now debunk the myth that it was used as a place of human sacrifice.

To the east of the Platform of Venus is the striking **Templo de los Guerreros** (Temple of the Warriors). Named for the reliefs depicting thousands of Maya warriors, the temple also has numerous columns, reminiscent of a classical Greek edifice. On

Templo de los Guerreros

a platform above the columns, and now closed off to tourists, is a replica of the original carved Chac-Mool in reclining position, his belly hollowed into a bowl for offerings.

Reached through a colonnaded walkway abutting the Temple of the Warriors is what modern archaeologists have named the **Mercado** or Market, with the remains of steam baths and a number of ball courts. Just south of the market are the tracks of the modern road (now diverted) that once cut through the site. Beyond this are more ruins to the south and west. Directly ahead is the **Tumba del Gran Sacerdote** (Tomb of the High Priest) which served as a tomb for one of the city's rulers. **Casa de los Metates** (the House of the Grinding Stones) is named after the corn-grinding stones of the Maya, which are used in villages in the region in the present day. Several were found here when archaeologists investigated the building. **Chichan-chob** (Little Holes, also called Red House) is an older-style building in the Puuc style. It has small holes in the roof and masks of Chaac-Mool on the upper walls.

Beyond a small ball court, you will see the imposing building of the observatory, **El Caracol** ⓱. An important place for the inhabitants of the city, observations taken here would predict the exact times of the equinoxes and

Hidden chamber

Maya pyramids were built in layers and inside El Castillo are the foundations of an earlier structure. So while it is no longer possible to climb the steep staircases to the upper platform on the outside of the pyramid, you can go inside, climbing the steps up to the inner chamber near the top. This once contained a jade-decorated jaguar and a Chac Mool statue. The originals are now to be found in Mexico City, but a replica of the jaguar statue can be seen.

Tzompantli – Wall of Skulls

important celestial events. El Caracol means 'the snail' in Spanish; it was given its name by explorer John Lloyd Stephens because he thought that the spiral staircase on the inside of the dome mimicked the chamber of a snail shell.

Edificio de las Monjas (Edifice of the Nuns), lying farthest south, is perhaps the most Puuc in style (see page 72) of all the buildings here. It stands on the site of much older buildings that can be seen in the interior. Nearby is a building called, surprisingly, **La Iglesia** (The Church). It isn't a place of Christian worship – in fact it is one of the oldest buildings on the site, and pays homage to the *bacah*, a group of gods thought to have held up the sky. Images of snail and tortoise can be seen here, among others. The walls of **Akab Dzib**, the Temple of Obscure Writing, to the east of the Church, are filled with Maya glyphs, the written language of the people that has been the focus of much attention and research in the last 30 years.

IZAMAL

Farther west, and north of the main highway, is the historic colonial town of **Izamal** ⑱. Known as the 'yellow city' because all the buildings on its main streets are painted the same yellow color, Izamal was once also an important Maya center and has recently been designated one of Mexico's 'magic' pueblos. There is a museum in the town, as well as a day spa and various restaurants.

At the heart of the city is the **Monastery of San Antonio de Padua**, home to the Franciscan order and founded by Archbishop de Landa in the 16th century. Today there are 10 monks continuing the tradition, though only their inner sanctum is out of bounds, leaving you free to explore the small courtyards and chapels. In 1993, Pope John Paul II visited the monastery to crown Our Lady of Izamal, Queen and Patron of the Yucatán.

The monastery and buildings on the surrounding streets have all been well-preserved, affording the visitor a unique view of a traditional colonial town. You can take a *calesa* ride through the quiet streets. The main Maya structure in Izamal is **Kinich Kakmo** ('the face of the maker of the sun'). With its base covering an entire block almost 200m (219 yds) square, and topped by a smaller pyramid, this is in fact the largest known structure of the entire Maya world. There are superb views of Izamal and its surroundings from the top.

MÉRIDA

The largest city in Yucatán and the capital of Yucatán State, **Mérida** ⑲ was founded in the 1540s, at the very start of the Spanish occupation, on the site of a large Maya city, T'Hó. Mérida became the focus of influence for the Montejo family, who exerted their force over the surrounding countryside. Since that time, it has seen the ebb and flow of economic prosperity and political power. Its architecture and lifestyle – a total contrast to modern Cancún – make it a fascinating place to visit. Mérida is a vibrant, bustling city with a tangible energy.

The heart of the city is the **Plaza Grande** (also known as the Zocalo). Its tree-lined center has shaded seats where residents come to meet and talk. Shoe-shine stands dot the walkways and vendors wander the plaza selling wooden toys and hammocks. Look for the *confidantes*, white love seats where courting couples could sit next to each other without compromising the woman's reputation. In the center of the square is a flagpole supporting a Mexican flag, which is raised and lowered at the start and end of each day (7am and sunset) in a typical Mexican ceremony performed by the local police band. Numerous historic buildings, dating back to the very earliest days of Spanish rule, line the square and its surrounding grid of streets. Construction of many of these buildings used stones from the Maya city of T'Hó, so, alas, nothing remains of this site today.

One of the city's important buildings is on the south side of the square. **Palacio de Montejo** was built as a family home for the Montejo dynasty and was completed in 1549. The facade – now the only original element of the house – is decorated with a number of ornate carvings, including two large conquistadors seen treading on the heads of Maya Indians.

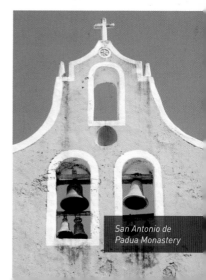

San Antonio de Padua Monastery

Perhaps this decoration was added to reaffirm Montejo power in the region. The style of the house is pure Spanish-colonial, with an inner courtyard garden lined by rooms with high ceilings and huge wooden doors. The house was in the Montejo family until the 1970s but then passed into the hands of a bank and later transformed into Museo Casa Montejo (Tue–Sat 10am–7pm, Sun until 2pm; free) housing four rooms furnished with 19th century Mexican furniture and three exhibition rooms.

On the west side of the square is the **Ayuntamiento** (City Hall). Inside you can see the wood-lined Sala de Cabildos, where the board of the city still holds its regular meetings. The northern side of the square is taken up by the **Palacio del Gobierno** (Governor's Palace; daily 8am–9pm; free), now merely an administrative building, but once the Governor's

Palacio del Gobierno

residence. There is a tourist information office just inside the entrance and in the inner courtyard hang many large canvases by local artist Fernando Castro Pacheco, illustrating important incidents and individuals in Yucatán's history. On the second floor, the Salon de Historia, a long gallery once used for social soirées, has more paintings that complete the collection.

The eastern side of the square is dominated by the **Catedral** (1561), one of the oldest in the Americas. Inside you will find the large crucifix christened **Cristo de las Ampollas** (Christ of the Blisters), which has been on display here since 1645. It was carved in the 1500s out of wood from a miraculous tree, so called because it had caught fire but did not burn. Later the finished crucifix survived another disastrous fire, though its surface was blistered. A few blocks away in the renovated Post Office building on Calle 65 is the **Museo de la Ciudad** (Tue–Fri 9am–6pm, Sat–Sun 9am–2pm), which displays drawings, maps, plans, photographs and interesting relics relating to the history, planning and growth of Mérida.

Next to the Catedral is the **Museo MACAY** (Museum of Contemporary Art; Wed–Mon 10am–6pm), which occupies a colonial building that once served as an armory. The gallery exhibits some interesting works of modern art, with permanent exhibitions of Yucatecan and other Mexican artists and a comprehensive program of temporary exhibitions.

The Plaza Grande occupies a square between calles 60 and 62 and calles 61 and 63 (even street numbers run east–west, odd street numbers run north–south); the surrounding streets boast numerous colonial gems that can only be appreciated by strolling around the town. For those with little time to spare, **Calle 60** has the most concentrated collection.

One block north of Plaza Mayor along Calle 60, you will pass **Parque Hidalgo**, dominated by the Jesuit-built church, La

Tercera Orden. Built in 1618, this church contains a painting that depicts the meeting in 1546 of Montejo and Tutul Xiú, the Maya ruler, who became a convert to Christianity, thus inducing most other local chiefs to follow his lead.

Beyond the church is another small square, **Plaza de la Maternidad**, which has a sculpture of *Mother and Child*, a copy of the Renoir piece in Paris. The **Teatro Peón Contreras** occupies the northern corner of the square. The theater, which has a regular schedule of performances, is a splendid example of late 19th- to early 20th-century architecture, with a sweeping marble staircase leading to a colonnaded upper balcony. It has a Parisian-style café on its first floor and there is a popular art gallery downstairs, to the left as you enter the building. There is another smaller gallery whose entrance faces the plaza. Across the street is the **Universidad de Yucatán**.

One block farther north is **Parque Santa Lucía**, with an array of busts in 'Poet's Corner' commemorating Yucatán's cultural and artistic contributors. Live bands and salsa dancing take place on the stage in this park on Thursday nights and Sundays.

City of culture

Mérida and culture go hand in hand. The city holds artistic and folkloric performances on every night of the week and an 'all-day' event in the heart of the city on Sundays. See the 'What to Do' section (see page 81) for more details.

If you are walking, make a right at Calle 47 past Parque Santa Anna, then left at the traffic circle. This is **Paseo Montejo**, one of the finest streets in the city, known by citizens of Mérida as 'the Champs-Elysèes of Yucatán.' This tree-lined avenue was *the* place to live during the 19th century, and all the best families and rich henequen

Houses on Paseo Montejo

producers vied for the best plots along its length. The houses they built still have an elegance and stature, though many have been lost to modern development.

The most impressive of the remaining period buildings is Palacio Canton, which now houses the **Museo Regional de Antropología e Historia** ⑳ (Regional Anthropological and History Museum; Tue–Sun 8am–5pm). The beautiful plasterwork detail and marble floors of the palace are only surpassed by the wealth of Maya artifacts on display. The displays illustrate the most recent theories on Maya society including trade patterns and social customs. On the second floor of the museum, exhibitions rotate, but are somehow related to the history and culture of the area. The museum is an excellent starting point for your tour of the Maya sites.

North from the museum, at a major intersection on the Paseo, is the **Monumento a la Patria** (Monument to the Fatherland, or

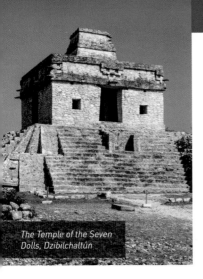

National Monument). This huge limestone monument depicting Maya, Spanish, and Mexican themes was begun in 1944 and completed in 1956.

DZIBILCHALTÚN

Although the Maya city of T'Hó has been swallowed by colonial Mérida, a 10-minute taxi ride north of the city is **Dzibilchaltún** (daily 8am–5pm), a city that thrived from 3000 BC on a marine economy – the coast being only 32km (20 miles) away. Archaeologists believe that at its peak in the late classic period (AD 600–800) the population reached 20,000.

The Temple of the Seven Dolls, Dzibilchaltún

El Templo de las Siete Muñecas (called the Doll's House, in English) is the most interesting structure at the site; it is the only Maya building with windows to be found so far, though these are not thought simply to have provided light for the room. The openings together with the doors frame the five segments of the sky marked by the solstices, the equinoxes and the zenith. When archaeologists were excavating the building they found seven small clay dolls, each with a bodily deformity. No one is sure whether these were simply a child's toys or if they had a religious significance, but they gave the structure its name. The dolls are on display in Mexico City, but facsimiles are displayed in the excellent museum found just beyond the site entrance.

To the north of Dzibilchaltún, at the end of Highway 261, lies **Progreso**, the closest beach town to Mérida and a popular spot to head for. It is an important fishing and container port, and also one of the newest ports for large cruise ships.

⊙ ECO-ATTRACTIONS IN THE NORTHERN YUCATÁN

There has been a great deal of development in the northern Yucatán during the last 40 years. But with acres of forest, coastline and lagoons, along with thousands of *cenotes* and hundreds of caves, it is no surprise that the area has a number of national parks and protected sites offering the opportunity to explore pristine natural environments.

North of Isla Mujeres is the tiny **Isla Contoy**, which is a bird sanctuary and wildlife preserve with large populations of gulls and frigate birds. You can reach it by boat from Isla Mujeres.

Río Lagartos on the coast north of Valladolid is a large lagoon and mangrove swamp, the breeding-ground for a huge flock of Caribbean flamingos. It also has small populations of crocodile, deer, boar and jaguar.

Celestún to the west of Mérida has the vast **Celestún Wildlife Refuge**, a protected feeding ground for the Caribbean flamingos, along with a myriad of other sea birds.

South of Tulum is the huge **Sian Ka'an Biosphere Reserve**, at 6,000 sq km (2,300 sq miles), the largest in the region. Much of this area, with mixed environments of mangrove, savanna, *cenote* and coral reef, has no human population, making it a suitable environment for the endangered jaguar as well as monkeys, deer, wild pig, birds and mangrove-dwelling creatures. For tours of the reserve, visit the offices of the Sian Ka'an Biosphere Reserve in Tulum (www.visitsiankaan.com).

THE PUUC ROUTE

The region to the south of Mérida is known as the **Puuc** (pronounced 'pook'). It has the highest ground in Yucatán, the 'Sierrita Puuc' – a ridge of limestone hills 50m (150ft) in height, and thought to be the edge of a giant crater formed when a meteorite fell to earth millions of years ago. Today the land is home to communities of Maya farmers, but the jungle has relinquished a number of fine ancient sites to explore. These sites are called Puuc sites, and this name has also been taken to describe the characteristics of the architecture and design of the buildings here. The Puuc style is characterized by ornate decoration, with latticework carving on the lower facades and masks and carvings on the upper levels.

The Maya settlements of the region were very rich. The fertile land enabled several crops a year to be harvested, and the resulting surpluses allowed the community to support artisans such as stonemasons and to trade with other communities for goods and raw materials not naturally available locally.

On the route south from Mérida you'll travel through countryside once filled with haciendas (the Mexican version of plantations). When the henequen

Hacienda Yaxcopoil Museum

boom was at its height, the number of haciendas grew dramatically, but the system fell into decline for various reasons after 1925–1930. The hacienda consisted of a main house surrounded by its land, a factory and a village for the hacienda workers. This would include a school and a company store where workers were forced to buy their supplies. Many of the modern villages of this region have their roots in the hacienda system. As you pass through them you may see an old chimney breaking above the tree line, a sign that the village was once part of a hacienda.

HACIENDA YAXCOPOIL

Head out of Mérida on Highway 180 towards Campeche, but at Uman go south along the 261. At km 33, take the exit to Yaxcopoil, a small *pueblito* dominated on the right-hand side of the road by the enormous **Hacienda Yaxcopoil** ㉑ (www.yaxcopoil.com; Mon–Sat 8am–6pm, Sun 9am–3pm), an excellent hacienda museum. The buildings are well preserved, but not overly restored – it's as if time has stood still. The main building, entered through an archway, consists of two parallel ranges. In the left-hand range, with its high ceilings, is the office, the living room, reception room, bedrooms, bathroom, and chapel, all with original period furnishings. The other range houses the kitchen and dining room, as well as the Maya Room, where pieces of pottery and other finds from the small ruins scattered around the estate are on display. It's also possible to visit the machine house, complete with the original henequen-processing machinery. Surrounding the hacienda is a Maya village, its inhabitants' descendants of the Maya who once worked on the huge estate.

UXMAL

Uxmal ㉒ (daily 8am–5pm; admission fee includes sound-and-light show in English at 8pm daily except Sun when admission is free) is considered the jewel of Maya sites in Yucatán, its buildings richly decorated with elaborate carvings. At its peak between AD 600–900 it is said to have had a population of

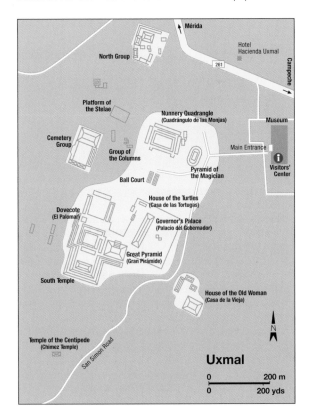

Mérida

Hotel
Hacienda Uxmal

261

Campeche

North Group

Platform of
the Stelae

Nunnery Quadrangle
(Cuadrángulo de las Monjas)

Museum

Cemetery
Group

Main Entrance

Group of
the Columns

Visitors'
Center

Ball Court

Pyramid of
the Magician

House of the Turtles
(Casa de las Tortugas)

Dovecote
(El Palomar)

Governor's Palace
(Palacio del Gobernador)

Great Pyramid
(Gran Pirámide)

South Temple

House of the Old Woman
(Casa de la Vieja)

N

Temple of the Centipede
(Chimez Temple)

San Simon Road

Uxmal

0   200 m
0   200 yds

Pyramid of the Magician, Uxmal

around 25,000 – remarkable when you consider that it had no water supply and had to collect and store water.

One of the highlights of the site presents itself immediately as you enter. The magnificent **Pirámide del Advino** (Pyramid of the Magician, also called the Pyramid of the Dwarf) sits atop five older structures. This pyramid is unique for a number of reasons. It has rounded sides, giving it a softened shape. It's steep (even more precipitous than the normal elevations in the area), and the design of the doorway at the top, which is a huge representation of Chaac, is found at no other site. The facade of the upper levels is extremely ornate and the main staircase has a parallel row of large Chaac masks. The pyramid has recently been restored, but as with El Castillo in Chichén Itzá, visitors to the site are now prohibited from climbing it.

Next to the pyramid is the **Cuadrángulo de las Monjas** (Nunnery Quadrangle), given its name in the 16th century because it resembled a Spanish monastery or nunnery. Its size – over 70 rooms – has caused archaeologists to postulate that it may have been a military academy, which expanded regularly throughout its history. The western building has the most richly carved facade. There are also numerous depictions of Maya homes or *na*, which can still be found all across the countryside of Yucatán. The eastern building has a statue of a dwarf dressed in a turtle shell placed in a position normally associated with the rulers of Maya cities. A serpent is entwined all along the upper facade around the statue. From its upper levels the many buildings at the site come clearly into view. The quadrangle is the setting for the **Uxmal Sound-and-Light Show**, which takes place every evening except Sunday.

South of the quadrangle, beyond a small ball court, the land rises to a higher level. Here another group of buildings forms the main center of focus at the site. The **Casa de las Tortugas** (Turtle House), so called because of numerous turtle motifs adorning it, is found immediately on the

⊘ THE SPEEDY LIFE OF THE DWARF

Maya legend has it that the dwarf who built the Temple of the Dwarf at Uxmal hatched from an egg and grew to adulthood during his first day of life. He spent his first night constructing the temple, which was complete by sunrise the next day.

Modern archaeological research is uncovering evidence that the dwarf of mythology may have actually been a real person – statues show a ruler who was short even by Maya standards – who could have contributed greatly to the building of this important city.

Uxmal Sound-and-Light show

right. Beside, and totally dwarfing it, lies the **Palacio del Gobernador** (Governor's Palace) with an imposing 100-m (320-ft) long facade. The building was erected in the 11th century for the ruler of the city, Halach Huinic ('the true man'), and consists of a central building flanked by two smaller wings. The frieze of Chaac masks is one of the most ornate and complex in the known Maya world.

Behind the palace is the **Great Pyramid**; it is less ornate than the palace, and only the front facade has been restored. Beyond this area, there are several other groups of buildings, many of which have yet to be excavated, including the Dovecote Group (which includes the **Casa de las Palomas**, the House of Doves) and the **Grupo del Cementario** (Cemetery Group). Beyond these are several even more remote sites that can be visited, but you would benefit from the services of a guide to find them.

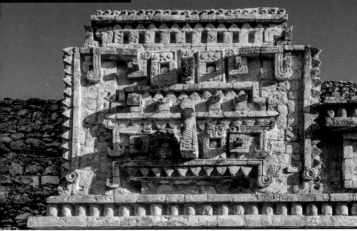

OTHER PUUC SITES

Uxmal was a very rich city at the height of its powers and protector of many smaller settlements, which paid tribute to it both in food and money. A string of these sites now forms what is called the Puuc Route, and they can all be visited in one day. Though small, each one has something different to reveal.

First in the tour is **Kabáh**, only 27km (17 miles) south of Uxmal. The major structure here is the **Codz-Pop** or Palace of the Masks, constructed in Chenes style – characterized by masks covering the whole facade of the structure from ground to roof. There are said to have been over 250 Chaac representations – a most impressive sight unique in the Maya world. Codz-Pop means 'rolled-up sleeping mat,' referring to the curled-up nose on the masks. Cross the main road dividing the site to find a restored archway, which once marked the end of a *sacbé* (sacred Maya road) from Uxmal.

Eight kilometers (5 miles) south of Kabah is **Sayil** ㉓, famed for its major building, called **El Palacio** (the Palace) by the Spanish. With over 100 rooms, it would be important for its size alone, but the ornate decoration makes it even more impressive, with representations of the Descending God found so prominently at Tulum.

Nearby **Xlapak** has only one major structure – a palace – but **Labná**, the final Puuc site on the tour, has a number of structures to explore. **El Palacio** here is decorated with alligators whose open jaws each have a human head emerging from them. This symbol, called Pop, is thought to be indicative of power and is only found at this site. A *sacbé* links the palace to other parts of the site. The tallest structure is the **Mirador**, a pyramid temple over 20m (65ft) high. Next to the Mirador is the most famous sight in Labná, also much changed since its discovery. **El Arco** (the Arch), is late Puuc style and was thought to have been the entrance to the courtyard of a family residence. Though the arch remains, two ornate walls at either side of it collapsed during the 20th century.

Before leaving the Puuc area, visit the **Loltún Caves** (tours daily at 9.30am, 11am, 12.30pm, 2pm, 3pm, and 4pm). On the guided tour through these impressive caverns you can see evidence of where the Maya rebels fortified the entrances during the War of the Castes in the 1840s.

THE CONVENT ROUTE

From the Loltún Caves, it's an easy detour north to **Maní**, where the Church of San Miguel Arcángel was the site of Bishop Diego de Landa's ritual burning of the Maya manuscripts in 1562. Mani is just one settlement along the so-called Convent Route, which you can follow by taking Highway 18 for the return to Mérida. There are a number of Franciscan-built monasteries and churches to visit, as well as the ancient city of **Mayapan**.

Cenote Choo-Ha near Cobá

WHAT TO DO

SHOPPING

Traveling around the Yucatán peninsula will present you with a wealth of shopping opportunities. Cancún has a number of modern, air-conditioned shopping malls, including La Isla Shopping Village, Plaza Kukulcán and Forum by the Sea (all in Boulevard Kukulcán), with internationally recognized brand names, where you can shop in comfort from morning to night, in some places at duty-free prices. For strolling and browsing in the Mexican sunshine or the cooler air of the evening, there are shopping streets in San Miguel de Cozumel, Isla Mujeres, the ruin and beach community of Tulum, the marina at Puerto Aventuras and on Avenida 5 in Playa del Carmen. These streets have stores selling locally produced crafts, jewelry and imported goods, as well as both boutique stores and those of internationally-known brands.

Visit the Ki Huic craft market in downtown Cancún, and better still the Mercado Municipal in Mérida, to experience the genuine, colorful atmosphere of a Mexican market. Examples of every locally-produced craft can be found in abundance in these markets. You can shop less expensively than in the resorts, negotiating prices and enjoy the local culture at the same time.

Don't let the range of goods blind you to low quality

Protected species

As you shop, be aware that certain items are made from protected species. It is illegal to sell tortoise-shell and black coral products, both of which are also illegal to import into Australia, the EU and the US.

or fakes. Always examine the item you want very carefully and shop around to get a feel of the prices before you buy. Most stores in the main tourist areas will stay open until 9 or 10pm. You can often pay in dollars at the resorts (but it's advisable to always pay in pesos not to lose money on the exchange), but in the local markets be prepared with small bills and change in pesos.

WHAT TO BUY

Handicrafts. The Maya people have always made everything they needed, and their handicrafts, though often practical, make beautiful souvenirs. Basketware made from sisal and other plants found in the area is typically used to carry a range of goods; woven mats can also be found. Hammocks come in a bewildering range of quality, colors and sizes; you'll have your choice of a *sencillo* (single) or one to share with friends, such as a *doble* (double) or *matrimonial* (family-sized). The tighter the hammock weave is, the better the hammock.

Weaving is an important Maya skill in other parts of Central America, but in the Yucatán the Maya practice the skill of embroidery. Maya women take great pride in embroidering the collars and hems of their white dresses, called *huipiles* with brightly colored floral designs.

Hammocks for sale on Isla Mujeres

Maya themes. The Maya have a special place in the imagination, and their traditional motifs and copies of their ceremonial artifacts make popular souvenirs. Carvings of the gods, Chac the rain god in particular, along with revered creatures such as the jaguar or the feathered serpent, are produced in stone, onyx, silver, wood and papier-mâché, in sizes from a lucky talisman for your purse to a sculpture for your garden.

Pottery and Ceramics. Pottery bowls, cups, masks and figurines are produced in various pueblos throughout Yucatán, but especially around the town of Ticul. These sculptural pieces are often replicas of pieces found throughout the area's archaeological sites.

Stone Sculpture. The Yucatán sits on a huge limestone shelf, which means that limestone, in many different colors and qualities, is easy to come by. Stonemasons sculpt the ubiquitous material into everything from bathroom sinks to small figurines. The larger pieces are difficult to take home, but smaller ones, from wind chimes and stone boxes to replicas of the Chichén Itzá Castillo, make great gifts. The town of Dzitya near Mérida is a pueblo full of stonemasons that sell their wares from the front yards of their houses.

Silver. Mexico is one of the largest producers of silver in the world. There is an amazing range of jewelry available, such as chains, earrings, and finger and toe rings, and prices are very competitive. Larger pieces such as tea-sets and goblets can be found in the bigger stores, as can silver pill-boxes, purses, or small 'sombreros.' Always make sure that your purchase bears a stamp of the word Mexico and of the numbers 925 (the standard quality of silver found here) or 960 (purer but slightly softer). This ensures that you are buying genuine silver.

Tequila and other alcohol. Tequila is the national drink of Mexico, made from the distilled juice of the agave plant (100%

agave tequila is the best quality) and it can be bought under numerous trade names. It is produced only in a very small region of Mexico, around the town of Tequila near Guadalajara and is in reality a refined version of the agave drink Mezcal. You can also take home a bottle of the Yucatecan liquor; Xtabentun (shtah-ben-toon), with its flavor of anise, honey and flowers.

Clothing. You are sure to find something that fits your personal taste in summer attire in the Yucatán. Designer labels from the US and Europe are abundant in the tourist-zone malls in Cancún and Playa del Carmen. Smaller stores throughout the region are filled with attractive beachwear, T-shirts, hats, footwear and cool, comfortable cotton dresses, skirts and sarongs that are ideal for the warm climate here.

Locally produced cottons and woven garments are sold in craft markets and stores. The colorful patterns have been handed down through the generations. In the countryside, the Maya women still wear the traditional *huipile*, a loose cotton slip

⊘ DUTY-FREE SHOPPING

Cozumel and Playa del Carmen are major cruise destinations and as such offer goods like fragrances and gemstones at duty-free prices. You can buy loose stones or finished pieces at a number of large, air-conditioned stores on Avenida Melgar, with prices said to be as much as 40 percent lower than US retail. If you intend to make a major purchase of this type while visiting the region, it would be wise to research the prices and quality of goods at home before you travel, so that you can be sure of getting a good deal. Cancún has luxury goods at lower prices due to a lower import duty and tax in that area.

with embroidered detail; the everyday version has stitching around the neckline and hem, the ceremonial version several layers of embroidery and lace. In Mérida, the men wear the *guayabera*, a short-sleeved linen or cotton shirt with finely pleated front detail, worn untucked. These tend to be much cooler than fitted shirts. *Huaraches* are hand-fashioned leather sandals with sisal thongs. You can top off your whole traditional ensemble with a hat: local people wear good quality hats made locally by artisans. You can also buy sombreros, though these are more traditional in regions of Mexico other than Yucatán.

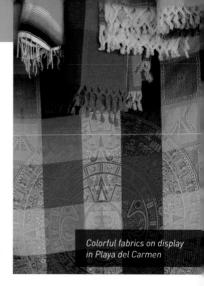

Colorful fabrics on display in Playa del Carmen

SPORTS

DIVING

Cancún, Cozumel and the Maya Riviera offer some of the most pristine waters for diving and a wealth of natural reefs and artificial dive sites to explore. They are still considered some of the best sites in the world, despite the explosion in the number of divers over recent years. The lack of soil and rivers on the Yucatecan mainland mean that there is no silt in the sea to reduce underwater visibility.

Cozumel is still regarded as the jewel among diving areas. There are 30km (20 miles) of reef at many different depths off the western coast. Divers have a chance to see turtles,

⊘ CHOICE DIVE SITES

COZUMEL

Palancar – Offers some of the best dive sites in Cozumel. Palancar Shallows is good for beginners, while Palancar Caves is a beautiful and interesting dive, but not for beginners.

Torments Reef – A wide swath of broken up reef, interspersed with sandy spots. The current can be strong here, but like many Cozumel dives, this is a drift dive so there is no need to swim against the current.

Yucab – South of Tormentos, Yucab is a haven for fish, lobster and crabs as well as brightly-colored coral.

Paso del Cedral Reef – A fairly shallow dive with good opportunities to photograph schools of fish. Moderate current.

PLAYA DEL CARMEN

Tortuga I – Drift dive off the coast of Xcaret. Divers here usually see multiple large turtles and sometimes large commuting deepwater fish.

Cerebros – Northernmost dive from Playa del Carmen. This shallow dive boasts large brain corals, swim-throughs and caves. Rays and barracuda are often found here, as well as many other colorful fish.

ISLA MUJERES

Manchones Reef – Just off the southeastern tip of the island, where the water is 5 to 11m (15-35ft) deep.

Banderas Reef – Stunningly beautiful colors and an abundance of marine life can be observed here at just 12m (40ft).

sharks and barracuda in their natural environment; the warm waters make for exciting and comfortable diving throughout the year. In addition, there are opportunities for both certified divers and those who would like to earn their certification.

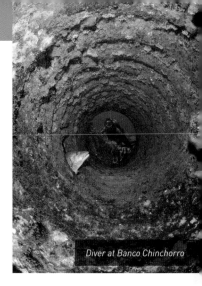

Diver at Banco Chinchorro

Cancún, Playa del Carmen and Tulum also have dive sites, including many shallow dive sites suitable for the novice. Experts can be well rewarded too – just a short distance from your hotel are challenging dive sites and some of the richest marine life on the planet. Remember to bring your dive certificate, as you will only be allowed to rent equipment and dive if you can prove your competence.

If you want to learn to dive along the Maya Riviera or on Cozumel, there is an excellent network of dive centers offering training to professional levels. All centers are affiliated with one of the major certifying bodies, NAUI (National Association of Underwater Instructors) or PADI (Professional Association of Diving Instructors), the latter being the most common. The basic qualification, the Open Water certificate, usually takes five days to complete. If you don't want to commit to a full diving course, many dive shops offer resort courses that allow you to go on shallow safe dives after just a day of training.

The following are a few of the many reputable dive centers in the area: **Scuba Cancún**, km 5 Kukulcán, Cancún, tel:

Flooded caves at Dos Ojos

(998) 849-7508, www.scubacancun.com.mx; Akumal Dive Center, Akumal, tel: (984) 875-9025, www.akumaldivecenter. com; **Deep Blue Dives**, A.R. Salas #200, Cozumel, tel: (987) 872-5653, www.deepbluecozumel.com; **Tank-Ha Dive Center**, Avenida 1 between 20th and 22nd Streets, Playa del Carmen, tel: (984) 873-0302, www.tankha.com.

SNUBA and SeaTrek at Xcaret (www.xcaret.com) and Xel-Ha (www.xelha.com) are half-and-half underwater experiences that let you breathe a constant supply of air through tubes at the surface.

SNORKELING

Well over half of all visitors to the region will snorkel while on vacation. The superb clarity and warmth of the water, the abundant sea life even in the shallows, and the proximity of all of this to the resorts are what make snorkeling here appealing. You can snorkel at just about every beach on the west coast of Cozumel, on Isla Mujeres and along the Riviera Maya. The many national parks offer more natural environments, though the sea may still be crowded with fellow snorkelers during the high season.

The inlets along the Riviera Maya are a perfect environment for small, brightly colored tropical fish. Xcaret is probably the most famous site, but you can enjoy snorkeling at Xel-Ha.

Many dive shops and beach clubs in Cozumel, Cancún, Isla Mujeres and Playa del Carmen rent snorkeling equipment so you don't have to buy your own.

CAVERN DIVING/SNORKELING

The freshwater *cenotes* and caverns of the peninsula offer another fascinating dimension to diving, and indeed snorkeling. A number of dive companies offer excursions and the most spectacular *cenotes* include Grand Cenote near Tulum and Cenote dos Ojos between Playa del Carmen and Tulum. Even novice snorkelers can admire the cavernous, crystal-clear depths here; for divers an open water certificate is sufficient. Aquaworld offers cavern and *cenote* diving in Cenote Dos Ojos, Cenote Tajma Ha and Cenote Chikin, www.aquaworld.com.mx. Other companies include Cancun Scuba Center, www.cancunscubacenter.com, and Scuba Diving Cancun, www.scubadivingcancun.com.

OTHER ACTIVITIES

Swim with the dolphins. These programs exist at various locations around the region. Some venues have a range of programs, from simply free-swimming with dolphins to performing exercises with them to helping a trainer for a day. Delphinus operates programs at Xcaret, Xel-Há, Cancún Interactive Aquarium and in some of the Riviera Maya hotels; www.delphinusworld.com. Dolphinaris programs can be found next to

Ventura Park in Cancún (www.dolphinaris.com), in Tulum and on Cozumel.

Viewing marine life without getting wet. If getting into the water isn't for you, then take a glass-bottom boat ride; trips navigate

⊘ BEST BEACHES

With over 14km (9 miles) of unbroken white sand, Cancún is famous for its beaches. The Riviera Maya has some of the most enjoyable beaches in the world, as do the islands off the coast:

Playa Tortuga, Cancún. Sheltered from the Caribbean waves by Isla Mujeres; great for snorkeling and swimming.

Playa Delfines, Cancún. One of Cancún's largest beaches with bright blue water, ideal for para-sailers and jet-skiers.

Playa Chaac Mool, Cancún. Close to all of the Hotel Zone's activities, bars and shopping.

Playa Norte, Isla Mujeres. At the northern tip of the island, with beautiful sand and shady palms.

San Francisco Beach and Playa Palancar, Cozumel. Both fine-sand beaches with good facilities and crystal-clear turquoise water.

Playa del Carmen. Eclectic and European. Topless bathing is common north of the Gran Porto Real.

Swimmers should beware of dangerous currents and undertows, particularly along the exposed stretches of coast. The local authorities have a code system, consisting of colored flags hung at public beaches and at major hotels:

White flag: Perfect or excellent conditions.

Green flag: Normal conditions; safe for swimming.

Yellow flag: Use caution; conditions changing or uncertain.

Red or black flag: Conditions unsafe for swimming.

the mangrove swamps or venture out to the ocean reefs. It is also possible to travel under the surface of the water in a submersible craft. Aquaworld offers many different sea-going adventures, including the SubSee Explorer. They can be found at km 15.2 Kukulcán Blvd in the Hotel Zone in Cancún, tel: (998) 848-8326/27, www.aquaworld.com.mx. Atlantis offers the Atlantis Submarine. You can find them on km 4 of

Jet skiers, Cancún

the Carretera, south of town opposite the Casa del Mar Hotel in Cozumel, tel: (987) 872-5671, www.atlantissubmarines.travel.

Watersports. Most of the major resorts will have water 'toys' for rent; you can jet-ski in the Caribbean or along the Mangrove swamps in the lagoon at Cancún. Note: Do obey the speed limits, which have been put in place to protect the delicate environment that is damaged by waves from speeding boats and jet-skis. And what better way to view the beautiful landscape, particularly the long beach and lagoon at Cancún, than from a parasail some 33m (100ft) up in the air? You'll be able to fully appreciate the color of the sand and the ocean from on high.

Sport fishing. The warm waters of the Caribbean are teeming with fish, and sport fishing is becoming increasingly popular. Large, powerful boats can be organized at just about every resort along the coast – they are particularly plentiful in

Cozumel and Playa del Carmen. The local guides are especially experienced and helpful. You can also go fly-fishing in the Nichupté Lagoon and the lagoons of the Sian Ka'an Biosphere Reserve, where catching four different types of fish (bonefish, permit, snook and tarpon) constitutes a so-called Grand Slam. Many operators practice catch and release, a technique that visitors are encouraged to request. Special hooks are available that ensure that the fish are not harmed.

Golf. Cancún has a growing number of golf courses, and the climate of the area is ideal for a round or two. Pok-Ta-Pok was the first course, and some still say the best. However, since it opened, several large hotels have built courses as part of their guest facilities: The Paradisus Cancún, km 16.5; The Iberostar Cancún, km 17; and The Westin Regina, km 19.5. There are several courses along the Maya Riviera, including the Five Diamond Mayakoba hotel, the Hard Rock Golf Club and the Iberostar Okaya Paraiso Golf Club in Playa del Carmen, with many more being built and in the planning stages.

Horseback riding. The Spanish introduced horses to the region, and they were perfect for transport through the 'low jungle.' Today you can explore the area on horseback, enjoying organized rides and guided trails and even ride

Birdwatching is popular in Río Lagartos

your horse on the beach at Loma Bonita Ranch on the main carretera between Cancún and Tulum.

Birdwatching. Protected lagoons and mangroves at Río Lagartos and Celestún, as well as many untouched jungle areas, provide havens for a wide variety of birdlife in the Yucatán. A popular inland spot for birdwatching is Hacienda Chichén, a hotel which practices sustainable tourism, and where over 150 species have been spotted (www. haciendachichen.com). Each year birders gather in the Yucatán from around the world for the Toh Bird Festival, a 3-day event, hoping to spot birds such as kingfishers, herons, egrets, ospreys, hawks and many more. For more details on birdwatching tours and events, see page 124.

ENTERTAINMENT

Before you head straight into the resort atmosphere of Cancún, check out what's happening in your hotel. Many have 'Las Vegas style' floor shows, Mexican evenings with traditional folk music and dances, and clubs where you can take to the dance floor yourself.

Cancún is developing so quickly that the latest hotspots change constantly. Ask your concierge where the place to be is, or just follow the crowds along the strip. Paseo Kukulcán in downtown Cancún has a collection of bars and clubs. On weekends you can join the locals in the Parque de Palapas, where the strains of rock, salsa and folk music can blend together into a bewildering cacophony.

If you choose to stay outside Cancún, things will be more laid-back, but no less entertaining. Cozumel has music bars along Avenida Melgar, and Playa del Carmen has bars and entertainment all along 5th Avenue and on the beach.

Fiestas

The Spanish colonists carried on the traditions of their mother country, and to this day there are yearly fiestas in most major towns. Many mark saint's days or founding days, and the whole population will dress up and enjoy lots of singing and dancing. Most have a religious procession to start the proceedings. The major fiestas are listed in the Calendar of Events (see page 96), but ask the tourist information office about what's going on during your stay.

The city of Mérida seems to be in the throes of a constant fiesta, hosting live cultural shows at sites around the downtown area. The program changes nightly from ballet to traditional Yucatecan folk music and dances, and all the shows are free. There are special performances on the famed Mérida en Domingo (Mérida on Sunday), lasting all day except for a short break in the heat of the afternoon, and coinciding with a huge artisans' market. On Sunday evenings Mexican families take to the streets to meet friends and family, dance, and generally have a good time. For a listing of events during your stay, visit the weekly events calendar on the Yucatán Living website www.yucatanliving.com.

ATTRACTIONS FOR CHILDREN

Mexicans love children, and will dote on yours. Kids are always welcome in restaurants and cafés. There are also many attractions and activities in the region to keep them happy.

Beaches. The beaches on the western coast of Cozumel or in Progreso and surrounding towns offer calm, warm water with generally benign conditions. In many places there are beach clubs with restaurants, restrooms and showers. Older children can enjoy snorkeling just offshore.

Submersible rides. Even very young children can safely see the fish and other marine life from inside a mini-submarine.

Boat trips. A day trip in a boat from Cancún to Isla Mujeres, or simply a trip around the coast or through the mangrove swamps can be a great adventure.

Crococún Zoo. Just ten minutes south of Cancún is a family-run zoo and croc-odile rescue center (http://

Mayan dancer in traditional costume

crococunzoo.com). Even small children can touch and feed baby crocodiles, spider monkeys and parrots.

Cancún Interactive Aquarium. Children can swim in the water with dolphins and sea lions and even observe tiger sharks. (www.interactiveaquariumcancun.com).

Xcaret. Superb beach, swimming lagoon, safe snorkeling, animals, horseback riding, turtles and an underground river.

Calesa rides at Mérida and Izamal. Young and old alike enjoy touring the town in a small, horse-drawn buggy.

Parque Zoológico del Centenario. On the outskirts of downtown. Open every day but Monday, admission is free.

Fiesta celebrations. Youngsters will be very welcome at any Mexican celebration.

Ventura Park in Cancún. Water slides and wave machines when you can't bear another beach day (www.venturapark. com).

CALENDAR OF EVENTS

January. *Año Nuevo* (New Year's Day): Religious festivals, parades, fireworks; new tribal leaders inaugurated throughout the Yucatán. *Three King's Day* is celebrated on the 6th.

February. *Carnival:* Week-long celebration leading up to Lent; parades, floats and dancing in Cozumel, Playa del Carmen and Mérida.

March. *Spring Equinox*, Chichén Itzá: Around the 21st, the spring sun aligns with the carved snake's head at the Temple of Kukulkán and fertilizes the earth for another year. *Easter:* The week before Easter is celebrated with reenactments of the events leading up to Christ's death. Processions and church services.

April. *Torneo Internacional de Pesca Deportiva*, Cozumel; Sport-fishing tournament takes place during the last week of the month.

May. *Labor Day:* Workers hold parades on the 1st. *Cedral Fair*, Cozumel: The anniversary of the first Catholic Mass celebrated in Mexico; cattle races and rides, bullfights held on the 1st–3rd. *Jazz Festival*, Cancún: dates vary.

June. *San Pedro y San Pablo*: Religious day of St Peter and St Paul; craft fairs and funfairs on the 29th.

September. *Fiesta de Independencia National* (Independence Day): National festival. *Fiestas de San Miguel Arcangel*: fiestas honoring the patron saint of Cozumel. *Fiesta del Señor de Las Ampollas* in Mérida (last week of September into October): Procession in the name of 'Christ of the Blisters.'

October. *Fiesta del Cristo de Sitilpech*: A figure of Christ is carried from Sitilpech almost to Izamal.

November. *Día de los Muertos/All Saints Day and All Souls Day*: National celebration of the dead on the 1st–2nd. *Ironman Cozumel* takes place late in the month. *Día de la Revolucion Mexicana Parade*, Cozumel: Revolution Day parade.

December. *Día de la Virgen de Guadalupe* (Day of the Virgin of Guadalupe): Religious processions followed by races. *Feast of the Immaculate Conception*, Izamal: Religious festivals and procession on the 3rd–9th.

EATING OUT

If you eat Mexican style, you may have to turn your normal pattern upside down. *El desayuno* (breakfast) is generally served from 7am–11am, and *la cena* (dinner) from 7–10.30pm, while *la comida* (lunch), the main meal of the day, is a movable feast eaten any time between noon and 4pm, traditionally followed by a siesta. However, in the easy-going atmosphere of Cancún and the other resorts, any time is mealtime. Many restaurants are open all day (a few are open 24 hours), and you can easily find a place to eat any time between 7am and midnight. There are the ubiquitous fast-food outlets in Cancún, Playa del Carmen and Cozumel, so you don't have to go without your favorite burger, though you probably won't miss it if you do. Tex-Mex and snack foods are also easy to find.

BREAKFAST

Most hotels and most restaurants offer a choice of American, Continental, or Mexican-style breakfast – Mexicans eat a large breakfast, especially on Sundays. A breakfast favorite is *huevos a la Mexicana*, eggs scrambled with a mix of onion, tomato and chili peppers. *Huevos rancheros* are fried eggs on a bed of tortilla and refried beans with a tomato and chili sauce. Eggs also come scrambled with spicy sausage (*chorizo*).

CLASSIC MEXICAN DISHES

Mexican cuisine is the result of blending the indigenous Aztec and Maya culinary traditions with the Spanish and Middle-Eastern influences introduced by the conquistadors and allowing the mixture to simmer for 400 years. Yucatecan cuisine is very different from traditional Mexican fare and can generally only be found in this part of Mexico. While in the parts of Yucatán which cater to tourists you can find enchiladas or *huevos rancheros*, most local restaurants will only be serving Yucatecan specialties.

The food basics that the Yucatán shares with the rest of Mexico are the staples – corn, beans and chilis. In the Yucatán, those ingredients are mixed with local ingredients such as *naranja agria* (bitter orange) and *habanero* chilies to create a cuisine that is unique.

Maíz, or corn, can be eaten on the cob (known as *elote*), but is principally used as cornmeal for making tortillas, the round, flat bread that accompanies almost every Mexican meal. Dried corn is boiled with lime to loosen the tough skin, then the cooked kernels are dried and ground into flour. The flour is mixed with a little water and patted out by expert hands into thin pancakes about 15cm (6ins) in diameter. These days, a tortilla press does the job more quickly and efficiently, but you will still see women making tortillas by hand at market stalls and in some tourist restaurants. Don't pass up the chance to eat a handmade tortilla, as they taste very different and are quite delicious.

Tacos in the Yucatán are generally open-faced tortillas, topped with shredded or sautéed meat of some kind, and often accompanied by pickled pink onions, a Yucatecan specialty called *cebollas en escabeche*, and black beans. *Enchiladas* are baked stuffed tortillas covered with sauce, and are not part of the traditional Yucatecan fare. Tortilla chips, known locally as *topos*, are often served with guacamole or ceviche (pickled fresh fish). *Chilaquiles* are fried tortilla strips and meat filling, layered in a casserole and baked. *Quesadillas* are not common in the Yucatán but can be found

---

Whatever you eat...

Enjoy your meal – **Buen provecho** (bwen proveycho)

Enjoy Mexican specialties

in tourist restaurants, and are tortillas topped with melted cheese and sometimes chicken or vegetables.

Frijoles, or beans, are usually of the red kidney variety (though in the Yucatán they are black) and turn up in soups and stews. But you will come across them most often in the form of *frijoles refritos* (refried beans), a tasty accompaniment to most traditional Mexican dishes. Refried beans are made by boiling the beans until they are tender, then mashing them into a paste in a frying pan with sautéed onion, garlic, and chili.

The ingredient that usually first springs to mind when one thinks of Mexican cooking is the chili pepper. However, it is wrong to think that all Mexican food is stoked to a fiery heat with red-hot chilies – or indeed that all peppers are themselves hot. Peppers have been cultivated in Mexico since prehistoric times. Today there are estimated to be between 60 and 100 different varieties throughout the world, from the large, sweet

Add to taste

Each restaurant makes its own sauces and strengths do vary – always test them out before adding them to your food!

red and green bell peppers in your local supermarket to the tiny, excruciatingly hot *prik khii nuu* chilies from Thailand. Among the more common varieties you will encounter in the Yucatán are the large, red, wrinkly *ancho* with a rich, mild flavor and the hotter *serrano*, which is smooth, green and tapered. *Chipotle* chilis are a common ingredient and are a smoked *jalapeño* pepper. They impart a very distinctive taste to any dish, and are flavorful and quite spicy. The local Yucatecan chili is the *habanero*, the hottest chili in the world. It is lantern-shaped, about 4cm (1in) long, and can be green, yellow, orange or red, depending on how ripe it is. *Habaneros* have a very distinctive flavor.

Despite its reputation, Mexican food is generally not as piquant as you would expect. It is usually cooked with mild spices and served with a number of pepper or hot paprika sauces that you then add to taste. No Mexican feast would be complete without a stack of warm tortillas and a dish or two of these sauces. *Salsa cruda* displays Mexico's national colors of red, white and green in a blend of chopped tomato, onion, chili and fresh cilantro (coriander), while *guacamole* is a delicious blend of finely chopped avocado, tomato, onion, garlic, chili and cilantro. A local specialty is *X'ni–pec* (shnee-pek), a Maya phrase literally translated as the 'dog's nose' because it makes your nose wet. It is a very hot sauce made with *habanero* chilies, onion, tomato, cilantro and lime juice. Beware – some of these sauces can be hot enough to make you see stars.

Perhaps the most famous of all Mexican dishes, normally reserved for fiestas but available in some restaurants, is *mole poblano*, a stew of chicken, turkey or sometimes red meat in a richly flavored sauce of tomatoes, chilies, garlic, nuts, spices and chocolate, which is reputed to have been served in the palace of Moctezuma, the Aztec emperor. Another classic is *pescado a la Veracruzana*, or fish Veracruz style. The fish is traditionally red snapper *(huachinango)*, or grouper *(mero)*, surrounded by a fragrant sauce of tomatoes, onions, capers and olives; scented with cinnamon.

SPECIALTIES OF YUCATÁN

The first surprise you may have after you arrive in Cancún is that your ideas about Mexican food will be radically altered. Mexico is such a big country that each of its regions has its own cuisine. The Yucatán is one of the more remote of these

Seafood taqueria, Mérida

Salbutes

regions, and its cuisine has developed to create a number of unique dishes, combining Maya, Spanish, Caribbean and European influences. The countryside of the Puuc region is known as the 'garden of the Yucatán', producing delicious vegetables and fruit. The indigenous cuisine or *cocina típica* makes much use of local ingredients such as sour oranges, limes, cilantro, honey and *habanero* chilies, along with onion and tomatoes that taste much more delicious than those at home. Any dish described as 'a la Yucateca' will have ingredients marinated or cooked in achiote; the ground seeds of the local annatto tree mixed into a paste with cumin seeds, garlic, peppercorns and sour-orange juice.

Traditionally the people of the Yucatán have eaten chicken, turkey and pork because, until recently, very few cattle were raised in the area. Today you can find beef on the menu, especially steak, which many say matches US beef in quality and taste. Filet mignon is available, but the most popular cut is *arrachera*, a skirt steak.

Classic Yucatecan dishes are *sopa de lima,* a hearty soup of chicken, vegetables and crisp-fried tortilla strips flavored with lime juice; *pozole,* a thick stew of turkey and vegetables; *poc chuc,* thinly cut pork marinated in achiote paste; and *pavo en relleno negro,* turkey and corn dumplings boiled in a burned *chili de árbol* sauce. Do not be discouraged by the black, oily appearance; it is a unique taste treat. *Pollo píbil* is chicken marinated in achiote paste and sour-orange sauce, baked in banana leaves; píbil means underground, and this dish was, until recently, cooked in earth ovens. The local people say it tastes much better cooked the traditional way, but today most restaurants slow-cook it in a normal oven. *Cochinita píbil* is pork cooked in the same way.

Some Yucatecan variations on the taco are *panuchos,* tortillas stuffed with black-bean paste, fried and topped with chicken, onion and tomato; *salbutes,* tortillas topped with shredded chicken or turkey; and *papadzules,* tortillas stuffed with hard-boiled egg with a sauce of tomato and onion spiked with chili and ground pumpkin seeds. You will also find *tamales,* cornmeal steamed in banana leaves, which can be either savory, with chicken or turkey meat and tomato sauce, or sweet, with sugar or fruit compote.

Don't miss the chance to sample the succulent Caribbean seafood. Fish in all varieties is served plain grilled or breaded. Shark meat is very popular in the Yucatán and is stewed or cut into steaks. *Langosta* (lobster) and *camarónes* (shrimp) are delicious simply grilled, or fried and served with garlic sauce. Conch (an abalone-like shellfish), shrimp and whitefish, marinated and partially cooked by the acidity of lime juice, then seasoned with tomato, onion, chili and coriander, are the components of the popular appetizer called *ceviche.*

The usual way to round off dinner is with a platter of fresh, tropical fruit: sweet, juicy pineapple, refreshing papaya and melon, succulent mango and banana and tangy orange. For something more filling, try *arroz con leche* (rice pudding with raisins) or *flan* (crème caramel).

DRINKS

Mexican beer *(cerveza)* is excellent, and is exported all over the world. It comes in two varieties, light *(clara)* and dark *(negra)*, and has a higher alcoholic content than most North American beers. Labels to choose include Bohemia, Dos Equis, Sol and Corona. When chilled they are perfect for quenching one's thirst on a hot sunny day. You will find them served with a piece of lime, which imparts a slight 'tang' to the overall taste. Dark Mexican beers such as Leon Negra have a nuttier, fuller taste, but are also served chilled.

Imported wines are available in the better restaurants, but Mexican wine, from the vineyards of Baja in the northwest of the country, is well worth trying.

☉ JUGOS, AGUAS Y LICUADOS

Probably the most tempting drinks the Yucatán has to offer are its fresh fruit juices *(jugos* for straight juice and *aguas* when diluted with water and ice), including orange, mango, melon, papaya, grapefruit and pineapple. A variation for the non-citrus fruits are the *licuados* (milkshakes), with mango, pineapple and banana being the most popular. Juices and *licuados* are available at most restaurants, but there are also juice bars. For a truly mouthwatering choice, try Janitzio on Mérida's Plaza Grande, which also specializes in fresh fruit ices and sorbets.

The national liquor is tequila, a fiery spirit distilled from the fermented juice of the agave plant. It is traditionally knocked back neat, accompanied by a pinch of salt and a twist of lime, or sipped slowly in a margarita, a cocktail of tequila, triple sec, lime juice and crushed ice served in a salt-rimmed glass. Another popular cocktail is the *mojito*, a Cuban drink, which is a concoction of rum, soda

Homemade guacamole

water, sugar, lime and *yerba buena*, or fresh mint leaves.

Mezcal is a regional variation of tequila distinguished by the presence of a pickled *agave* worm at the bottom of the bottle. It may look off-putting, but the worm was traditionally added as a sign of quality – if the Mezcal was good the worm would stay intact, but if it was of poor quality the worm would rot in the bottle. Although there is no longer a need for this quality control mechanism, the worm stays by popular demand.

Kahlúa is a pleasant coffee-flavored Mexican liqueur, but a more exotic after-dinner drink is *xtabentún*, a Maya liqueur flavored with fermented honey, flower petals and anise.

Familiar brands of soft drinks *(refrescos)* are bottled under license in Mexico and are available everywhere, as is mineral water. For a delicious alternative to carbonated drinks, try freshly prepared juices and shakes. Two other popular Yucatecan thirst-quenchers are *horchata*, a concentrated rice, almond and cinnamon mixture to which you add water to taste, and *jamaica* (pronounced ha-MY-kah), a sweet tea made from hibiscus flowers.

Coffee is usually served black; if you want it with milk ask for *café con leche*. A spicy Mexican variation is *café de olla*, which is coffee brewed in a small earthenware pot (the olla) with cinnamon, cloves and hard brown sugar *(poncillo)*. *Té de manzanilla*, chamomile tea, is a refreshing change from coffee, and is known to be particularly good for settling an upset stomach. Some establishments will still serve *chaya* drinks, made from a vegetable like spinach used by the Maya in healing. You can take it as tea or mixed with lemonade as a cold drink.

TO HELP YOU ORDER...

Here are some select terms that will enhance your dining experience. Be bold and try to scrape by in Spanish – your efforts will be appreciated.

Do you have a table for one/two/three/four people? **¿Tiene una mesa para una/dos/tres/cuatro persona/personas?**
Do you have a menu? **¿Tiene un menú?**
The bill, please. **La cuenta, por favor.**

...AND READ THE MENU

aguacate avocado
ajo garlic
bistek steak
café coffee
calamares squid
camarones shrimp
cerdo/puerco pork
cerveza beer
ensalada salad

frijoles beans
huevos eggs
leche milk
mariscos seafood
mejillones mussels
papas potatoes
pescado fish
pollo chicken
queso cheese

PLACES TO EAT

Below is a list of restaurants throughout the region. As a basic guide we have used the following symbols to give some idea of the price of a three-course meal for two, excluding drinks:

$$$$$	more than US$60
$$$$	US$50–60
$$$	US$40–50
$$	US$30–40
$	below US$30

CANCÚN

Downtown

La Habichuela Centro $$$ *Calle Margeritas No. 25, tel: (998) 884-3158*, www.lahabichuela.com. Set in a Yucatecan home with authentic wooden floors, this small restaurant serves great combination Yucatecan-Caribbean dishes.

Labna $$ *Calle Margaritas No. 29, tel: (998) 892-3056*, www.restaurantelabna.com. The perfect place to try out exotic Yucatecan dishes in air-conditioned comfort. Traditional favorites include pibil pork, arrachera and chicken in mole. Mayan-themed interior. Open daily 1pm–midnight.

Yamamoto $$$ *Avenida Uxmal 31 esquina Rubia, tel: (998) 884-3366*, www.yamamoto-cancun.com. Cancun's oldest and most established sushi restaurant is also its best, serving a wide assortment of fresh and cooked fish, as well as other traditional Japanese dishes. Open Mon–Sat 1.30–11pm, Sunday 1.30–8pm.

Hotel Zone

Hacienda Sisal $$$ *Boulevard Kukulcán km 13.5, Hotel Zone, tel: (998) 848-8220*, www.haciendasisal.com. Inside includes traditional high ceilings, beveled glass doors and windows, and one of the rooms features a traditional handcrafted dome, all working together to create a romantic hacienda atmosphere. Traditional Mexican fare. Reservations required. Open daily 2–11pm.

Cenacolo $$$ *Boulevard Kukulcán km 13.5, Hotel Zone, tel: (998) 885-3603*, www.cenacolo.com.mx. One of Cancun's most established restaurants with a gourmet Italian and continental menu. Dine in casual elegance on authentic pastas, seafood, meat and pizzas. Pasta and bread are made on-site in an open kitchen. Imported wines. Open daily 2–11.30pm.

Puerto Madero $$$ *Boulevard Kukulcán km 14.1, tel: (998) 885-2829*, www.puertomaderorestaurantes.com. Authentic Argentinian steakhouse also serving fish and seafood. Dine indoors in an air-conditioned, wood-paneled room or outdoors on the deck overlooking the lagoon. Reservations recommended. Open daily 1pm–1am.

Johnny Rockets $ *La Isla Shopping Village, Boulevard Kukulcán km 12.5*, *tel: (998) 883-5575*, www.johnnyrockets.com. 1950s-style diner with great burgers and a wide choice of other treats. Open daily 9am–11pm.

La Dolce Vita $$$ *Av. Coba 87, tel: (998) 884-3393*, www.cancunitalian restaurant.com. Said to serve the best Italian food in Mexico, this restaurant is housed in a custom-made building overlooking the lagoon. Seafood is a specialty. Open daily 8am–11pm.

La Joya Restaurant $$$$ *Boulevard Kukulcán km 9, the Coral Beach Hotel, tel: (998) 881-3200*, www.coralbeachcancunresort.com. Superb restaurant serving the best in Mexican cuisine. The beautiful dining room is matched by the presentation and service. Good wine list. Open Tue–Sun 6.30–11pm.

Lorenzillo's Lobster House $$$$ *Boulevard Kukulcán km 10.5, tel: (998) 883-1254*, www.lorenzillos.com.mx. *Palapa*-style restaurant with a pretty terrace located by the shallows of the lagoon. The best in fresh seafood, but lobster is the specialty, served all year from the restaurant's lobster farm. Ribs and prime rib roast also on the menu. Open daily 1pm–midnight.

Mikado $$$ *adjacent to Marriott CasaMagna Resort, Boulevard Kukulcán km 14.5, tel: (998) 881-2000, www.mikadocancun.com.* Japanese and Thai cuisine; sushi, sashimi, teppan-yaki and fragrant Thai soups and curries. Individual tables or shared 'show' tables; features a terrace with spectacular lagoon views. Open daily 5.30–11pm.

Ruth's Chris Steak House $$$ *Boulevard Kukulcán km 13, tel: (998) 885-3301, www.ruthschris.com.mx.* Internationally acclaimed for its prime steak, cooked exactly to your requirements; also try seafood dishes such as the blackened tuna. Reservations recommended. Open daily 1–11.30pm.

Tempo by Martin Berasategui $$$$ *Boulevard Kukulcán km 16.5, at the Paradisus Hotel, tel: (998) 881-1100, www.tempocancun.com.* Delightful Spanish food prepared by acclaimed chef Martin Berasategui, awarded with eight Michelin stars during his entire career. Excellent seven-course tasting menu is really worth a try. Open daily 6–11pm.

ISLA MUJERES

Restaurant-Bar Amigos $$ *Avenida Miguel Hidalgo No. 19, tel: (998) 877-0624.* Good Mexican/international cuisine at reasonable prices. Tasty breakfasts. Indoor and outdoor seating; friendly service. Open daily 7am–10.30pm.

Casa Rolandi $$$$ *Carretera Sac Bajo, Laguna Mar, at Zoétry Villa Rolandi, tel: (998) 999-2000, www.zoetryresorts.com/mujeres.* Gourmet Swiss-Northern Italian cuisine. Tables indoors and outdoors. Open 24 hours.

La Cazuela M & J $–$$ *behind the church, off the main square, next to Hotel Roca de Mar, tel: (998) 877-0734, www.lacazuelamj.com.* A wide range of Mexican and international cuisine, specializing in cazuelas – a cross between an omelette and a soufflé. Indoor and outdoor seating; great views of the Caribbean. Open Wed–Mon 7am–2pm.

Oceanus $$$ *Zazil-Ha 118, at the Hotel Na Balam, tel: (998) 881-4770, www. nabalam.com.* The beautiful beach setting of this restaurant is matched by the delicious fresh food. A good range of dishes, from seafood and pasta to traditional Maya and Mexican. Open daily 6–11pm.

COZUMEL

Casa Denis $$ *Calle 1 Sur No. 132, Centro, tel: (987) 872-0067*, www.casadenis.com. Long-established restaurant in a traditional wooden clapboard house just off the main square, serving authentic Yucatecan food, tacos and seafood. Open daily 8am–10pm.

Guido's $$ *Avenida Rafael E Melgar 23 between calles 6 and 8, tel: (987) 872-0946*, www.guidoscozumel.com. Pizzas cooked in a wood-fire oven; succulent pastas served with a variety of sauces. The small entrance leads to a pretty, plant-filled courtyard. Open Mon–Sat 11am–11pm, Sun 3–9.30pm.

La Cocay $$$ *Calle 8 between Avenida 10 and Avenida 15, tel: (987) 872-4407*, www.lacocay.com. This modern gem of a restaurant is an unexpected surprise. If it wasn't for the tropical breezes and the Caribbean atmosphere, your tastebuds would think they were in New York. Open daily 5.30–11pm.

Le Chef Cozumel $$$ *5 Avenida 380 between calles 3 and 5, tel: (987) 878-4391*. Mexican restaurant specializing in seafood dishes. Lobster and bacon sandwich is a must. The establishment has a very nice garden at the rear for open-air dining. Open daily 8am–11pm.

Pancho's Backyard $$ *Avenida Rafael E Melgar 27, tel: (987) 872-2141*, www.panchosbackyard.com. Excellent Mexican and Central American dishes served at one of the most beautiful colonial buildings with a lovely patio. Open daily Mon–Sat 10am–11pm, Sun 4–11pm.

PLAYA DEL CARMEN

Café Tropical $$ Avenida 5 between Calle 8 and 10, tel: (984) 873-2111. Two-story restaurant serving fresh homemade food. Pastries, eggs, fruit dishes, smoothies, sandwiches and more. Sit upstairs for cooling breeze or downstairs for great people-watching. Open daily 7am–midnight.

Chiltepin Marisquillos $$ *Calle 34, corner of Avenida 20, tel: (984) 147-7287*. Nice restaurant serving Mexican and Caribbean fare including mouthwatering seafood. Octopus is particularly worth a try. Indoor and outdoor seating. Open daily noon–2am.

La Casa del Agua $$ *Avenida 5, corner of Calle 2, tel: (984) 803-0232,* www.lacasadelagua.com. Great fusion cuisine paired with excellent wines. Two-story open-air restaurant plus a wine cellar. Open daily 1pm–midnight.

La Parrilla $$ *Avenida 5, corner of Calle 8, tel: (984) 873-0687.* Long-established Mexican restaurant specializing in grilled seafood and meats. Open daily noon–2am.

Oh Lala! $$$$ *Calle 14 between Avenida 10 and Avenida 15, tel: (984) 127-4844,* www.ohlalabygeorge.com. International fare offered in a small restaurant so reservations are recommended. Open daily 6.30–10.30pm.

Puerto Cocina Urbana $$$ *Avenida 5 between calles 34 and 38, tel: (984) 147-3073.* Successful fusion of Mexican, Caribbean and Central American cuisines. Extensive Mexican craft beer menu. Open daily noon–midnight.

MÉRIDA

Restaurant Amaro $$ *Calle 59 between calles 60 and 62, tel: (999) 928-2451.* Pleasant courtyard restaurant serving vegetarian and whole-food dishes, along with crepes and Yucatecan specialties. Open daily 11am–1am.

Apoala Mexican Cuisine $$$ *Calle 60, tel: (999) 923-1979.* Hacienda-style dining. Traditional Mexican and fusion fare, full bar and laid-back atmosphere. Open Mon–Sat 1pm–midnight, Sun 2–11pm.

Kuuk $$$$ *Avenida Romulo Rozo 488, tel: (999) 944-3377.* Very good, beautifully presented Mexican dishes served in the lovely setting of an old house. Open Tue–Sat 1–11pm, Sun 1–5pm.

Muelle 8 $$$ *Calle 21 No. 141 between calles 30 and 32, tel: (999) 944-5343.* One of Mérida's best seafood restaurants, specializing in fresh Gulf and Caribbean fare and including such classics as *pescado a la Veracruzana* (fish Veracruz style). Open daily 1–6pm.

A–Z TRAVEL TIPS

A SUMMARY OF PRACTICAL INFORMATION

Note that the peso is signified by the $ sign, prices quoted in dollars by US$.

A

ACCOMMODATIONS (see also Camping, and the list of Recommended Hotels on page 135)

The first hotels in the Tourist Zone of Cancún did not appear until the early 1970s, and the proliferation of building since that time has seen over 150 hotels completed and more being planned. Rooms have in-suite cable TV and air-conditioning, and have a range of guest amenities such as pools, spas, and gyms, equipment for numerous watersports, and a number of golf courses. In some hotels these activities will be included in the price, though this is something you will need to confirm before you make a reservation. In downtown Cancún, you will find lower priced establishments and business-type hotels. These are a short car or bus journey from the beaches and will usually have basic, clean facilities.

On Cozumel and Isla Mujeres and along the coast of the Maya Riviera, there is a much wider range of accommodations. There are a few luxury hotels, but also many mid-range options and smaller, family-run hotels.

The high season in the resorts runs from December through April, the low season from September through December. Prices can vary by as much as 50 percent between high and low seasons. It is important to make a firm reservation if you intend to travel in high season.

In the countryside of the Yucatán, a number of old haciendas (plantation houses) have been transformed into hotels. Some market themselves as exclusive hideaways and can be expensive, but they do offer a unique experience to guests. Mérida has a range of hotels, B&Bs and vacation rentals ranging from budget to luxury.

You will find accommodations at all major Maya sites, most of which are less expensive than in Cancún. Always book in advance if you intend to say overnight, particularly in high season, as group bookings can completely fill hotels.

A tax is added to hotel prices throughout the Yucatán: this may or may not be quoted in the price, so always ask when you are given a room rate whether tax is included.

> I'd like a single/double room **Quisiera una habitación sencilla/doble**
> with bath/shower **con baño/regadera**
> What's the rate per night? **¿Cuál es el precio por noche?**
> Where is there a budget hotel? **¿Dónde hay un hotel económico?**

AIRPORTS *(aeropuertos)* (See also Getting There)

Cancún International Airport, 20km (12 miles) south of the city, is the second busiest airport in Mexico, handling almost 21.5 million passengers in 2016. It is both a domestic airport, and one that serves the entire Riviera Maya with international scheduled and charter flights. Facilities at the airport include a tourist information office, car rental agencies, duty-free stores, and restaurants and bars.

Your hotel may have a courtesy bus to pick you up at the airport; otherwise you can take a public ADO bus (www.ado.com.mx) which leaves the airport every half an hour and takes 20-30 minutes to get downtown (around $66) or one of private shuttle vans to the Hotel Zone or downtown (from $40). Taxi fares are around US$40–60 depending on the exact location of your hotel.

If you intend to travel from the airport to Isla Mujeres by boat, you will need to get to the Puerto Juárez passenger ferry. Minibuses can take you to the bus station downtown, and from there you can catch a minibus to Puerto Juárez. From the bus station there are regular services along Highway 307 to Playa del Carmen or Tulum and other places on the Yucatán Peninsula. Taxis are also available at the airport to take you anywhere in Cancún or on the Riviera.

A departure tax is levied on all flights. This is usually included in the price of the ticket, but if that's not the case the tax must be paid on departure in cash (either US dollars or pesos).

Cozumel has an international airport just 5 minutes north of San Miguel. It takes direct flights from destinations in the US, as well as on-ward flights from Cancún, Mérida, and Mexico City. A *colectivo* from the airport into town will cost around $10; a shared private van is around $15-25 and taxis are around $80-170 depending on the location of your hotel.

Mérida International Airport has a growing number of domestic and in-ternational flights and is located about 15 minutes from the center of town.

B

BUDGETING FOR YOUR TRIP

Prices in the resort areas of Cancún and Cozumel are generally higher than resorts in the US, but represent good value when compared with the UK and Europe. If you make a hotel booking as an individual, most rates will be quoted as European plan (just room), but you should be able to book American plan (room and meals) if you want. Many hotels operate an all-inclusive policy; one price covers room, food, drinks, and activities.

Archaeological sites. The entrance fee to most Maya sites is around US$5-7, though Chichén Itzá and Uxmal are more expensive, US$10-12. The light and sound shows at some of the sites cost extra. Children under 12 almost always go free; some sites have reduced admission on Sundays.

Ecoparks. The basic cost of entrance to ecopark attractions ranges from around US$89 (Xel-Ha) to US$99 (Xcaret) per person per day and up; children half-price.

Other Activities. 'Swimming with Dolphins' programs can cost up to US$150; two tank dive US$80-90; snorkel rental US$8-10; jungle tour on speedboat in the lagoon US$50-70; 30 minutes horseback riding US$25.

Bus. Hotel Zone to El Centro (downtown Cancún) $8.50; Cancún to Playa del Carmen $40.

Car rental. US$70–80 per day. You can usually get a car on Cozumel for US$50 a day and a golf cart rental on Isla Mujeres for about US$50 a day.

Ferry. Playa del Carmen to Cozumel US$10-15 one-way depending on the company; Cancún to Isla Mujeres US$7 single from Puerto Juaréz, US$15 from the Hotel Zone.

Meals. Dinner for one at a mid-priced restaurant US$20–30.

Taxi. Hotel Zone to downtown US$15.

Once out in the Yucatán – away from the main tourist areas – prices for most goods drop dramatically.

C

CAMPING

There are few opportunities for camping in the Yucatán, though RV parks can be found near Uxmal and Chichén Itzá, as well as along the coast around Playa del Carmen.

CAR RENTAL *(coches de alquiler)* (See also Driving)

Car rental in Mexico is expensive by international standards, but it is a good option if you intend to travel around the Yucatán from Cancún. Roads are generally in good condition and traffic is light – except in the downtown areas. It would not be wise to drive at night in the countryside, because the roads are rarely lit and animals do stray across them.

You will need to hold a current valid driver's license and be over 21 (25 for some agencies). National driver's licenses from all major countries are accepted when renting a vehicle. If you do not have a credit card, you will be required to pay a large cash deposit.

All the major international car rental agencies operate from the airports in Cancún, Cozumel and Mérida as well as downtown locations. Prices start from around US$50 per day for a compact Dodge or Chevrolet. This includes tax but not insurance, which runs around $15-20 per day. It pays to shop around. Watch out for terms of insurance – excess charges on fully comprehensive cover, for instance. You may get a better rate by the week and by pre-booking your rental car before you arrive in Cancún. Be aware that if you make a booking while in the resort, you will be given a quote in US dollars but charged in pesos.

Make a note of the telephone number of your car rental office just in case you break down. You can call them to arrange assistance. Exploring Cozumel is greatly benefited by having a vehicle of some kind, even if only for a couple of days. Prices are similar to those at Cancún, as are the rules governing vehicle rental.

Here are the websites for the major car rental agencies operating in the Yucatán: **Alamo**, www.alamo.com; **Avis**, www.avis.com; **Budget**, www.budget.com; **Dollar**, www.dollar.com; **Europcar**, www.europcar.com; **Executive**, www.executive.com. mx; **Hertz**, www.hertz.com; **Thrifty**, www.thrifty.com.

Exploring Isla Mujeres is fun, but the island is too small to warrant car rental. Alternative forms of transportation include: golf cart rental on Mujeres US$50 per day; moto (motor-scooter) US$25-30 per day; bicycle US$10 per day.

CLIMATE

The Yucatán has a tropical climate; the temperature therefore remains fairly constant throughout the year, and rarely falls below 27°C (81°F) during the day. Expect temperatures to reach around 33°C (92°F).

The year is split into two 'seasons': the dry, between December and mid-May, roughly coincides with the peak tourist season; the rainy, between mid-May and November, sees increased humidity but no decrease in temperature. Hurricane season falls between July and early November, and Cancún experiences a small number of tropical storms each year, though there is no regular pattern.

The following chart lists the average temperature for each month:

	J	F	M	A	M	J	J	A	S	O	N	D
°C	21	21	22	24	26	27	28	29	27	26	23	21
°F	70	70	72	75	79	81	82	84	81	79	73	70

CLOTHING

Cool and casual are the bywords for your trip to Cancún and Cozumel. During the day you will need only beachware, T-shirts and shorts for all the resort areas. Natural fabrics such as cotton and linen are the most comfortable in hot, humid climates. Sunglasses are important, especially on the beaches, where the pale sand reflects the sun's strong light. If you intend to travel inland to the towns and villages, and especially if you wish to enter churches, you should dress more conservatively. Always take a covering layer and a hat for archaeological sites – to avoid getting too much sun – and don't forget sensible footwear for climbing the temple steps.

As the sun sets, the mood remains casual – ties and jackets are rarely needed – but most people change into something informal or 'tropical' for dinner. A light sweater may come in handy for the odd cooler evening.

CRIME AND SAFETY (See also Police)

Generally, the Yucatán is a relatively safe place to visit, but still prone to some petty crime directed against tourists in and around the resort areas. Always watch your luggage at airports, getting into taxis and checking in and out of hotels. Use the hotel safe for all valuables, and do not leave anything on view in your rental vehicle. When sunbathing, don't leave valuables to go swimming. Report any theft to the police immediately. Keep to well-lit public areas after dark.

You will find specially trained 'tourist police' patrolling the streets of the city centers in Mérida and Izamal. You will be able to go to them with any problems that you may have; they all speak some English.

CUSTOMS (aduana) AND ENTRY REQUIREMENTS

American, Canadian and British visitors as well as visitors from the Schengen Area entering Mexico must have their passport valid for at least six months. These rules have been changing lately, so it is always best to check before traveling for the latest updates (e.g. http://travel.state.gov).

Though you don't need a visa, each traveler must carry a Mexican Visitor's Permit (FMM) while in the country. The permits are issued by the airlines, cruise companies and at border crossings, and are normally valid for 30 days but can cover periods of up to 180 days. Always make sure that your stamp covers the length of your stay. You must carry your permit with you and give it back to the customs agent when leaving the country.

Customs officials will want to be sure that you are not bringing goods to sell while you are in Mexico. Those with a large amount of luggage or unusual pieces are likely to be searched and questioned, but items such as golf clubs, scuba gear and camera equipment should be fine. You are also allowed to bring in 10 packs of cigarettes, 25 cigars or 200g of tobacco and three 1-liter bottles of alcohol (any strength) into the country.

Currency restrictions. Non-residents may import or export any amount of freely convertible foreign currency into Mexico, provided that it is declared on arrival. There is no limit to the amount of Mexican currency you may carry into or out of Mexico.

> I have nothing to declare. **Yo tengo nada que declarar.**

D

DRIVING

In Mexico, drive on the right and pass on the left. A lot of useful travel information is available from the US Department of State at https://travel.state.gov/content/passports/en/country/mexico.html.

Road conditions in most areas are perfectly adequate and always improving. Roads in the Cancún area are good; the major connecting highways down the coast to Tulum and across to Mérida are too. There is a toll road, the 180, from Cancún to Mérida (tolls are relatively high, so the highway is quiet), but it bypasses many settlements that offer fascinating insight into the lifestyle of the local people. Be aware that the incidence of traffic accidents in Mexico is relatively high so drive defensively.

In Cancún, traffic is controlled by traffic lights at intersections, but there are a number of traffic circles as well. Right of way goes to traffic already on the rotary.

Built-up areas and villages in the countryside have speed control devices, usually *topes*, speed bumps. They often come in series, so keeping your speed to a crawl is recommended to avoid damage to both car and occupants. There are also *topes* in downtown Cancún, marking the main pedestrian crossings on Avenida Tulum.

The narrow streets of San Miguel de Cozumel have their own set of rules. If you are traveling parallel to the sea, you have the right of way at all junctions. Those traveling east–west do not have right of way and should stop at every intersection. However, this is not general knowledge to visitors – so take extra care!

Rules and regulations. Speed limits are 30–40kmh (19–25mph) in towns, 60kmh (38mph) in the Hotel Zone, and 110kmh (69mph) on the toll road out of town.

Fuel costs. Pemex (Petroleras Mexicanas), a government-controlled company, has a monopoly on gas *(gasolina)* sales. They do not accept credit cards in payment. Gas is sold by the liter in lead-free (magna) and premium (premio or super). Pemex has done a good job of building gas stations around the Yucatán to anticipate the demands of tourists, so the chances of running out of gas are quite slim, but if you are planning a long trip, it's best to fill up just in case. Pemex stations are all full-service, and it is customary to tip the attendant $5–15 for their help.

Parking. Do not park where you see red lines on the kerb, or where there is a sign of an 'E' with a line through it. Most hotels have parking lots, but some charge for them. This is especially true in Mérida.

Road signs. Mexican road signs are the standard international pictographs, but you may also encounter these written signs.

Alto Stop
Ceda el paso Give way

Circulación Direction of traffic
Cruce de peatones Pedestrian crossing
Curva peligrosa Dangerous bend
Cuidado Caution
Cuota Toll
Desviacion Detour
Disminuya su velocidad Reduce speed
Escuela School
Peligro Danger
Prohibido estacionarse No parking
Prohibido rebasar No overtaking
Salida de camiones Truck exit
(International) driver's license **Licencia para manejar (internacional)**
Car registration papers **registro del automóvil**
Are we on the right road for...? **¿Es ésta la carretera hacia...?**
Fill the tank, top grade, please. **Llénelo, por favor, con super.**
Check the oil/tires/battery. **Revise el aceite/las llantas/la batería.**
I've broken down. **Mi carro se ha descompuesto.**
There's been an accident. **Ha habido un accidente.**
Could you mend this flat? **¿Puede arreglar este pinchazo?**

Bringing your car into Mexico. Although the Yucatán is a long way from the northern Mexican border, you may want to travel across country with your own vehicle. You will need a temporary importation permit, which can be obtained at any border crossing. This must be surrendered when you leave Mexico. A car importation fee must be paid by credit card (in the same name as the vehicle registration document). Car registration documents must be carried, along with a valid driver's license. You must sign a form promising to leave the country with your vehicle.

If you need help. A government-sponsored highway assistance service called Angeles Verdes (Green Angels) patrols the major highways every day. They offer free roadside assistance (though you will have to pay for parts) as well as information, and they speak English. Use the Mexican emergency number 066 or 911 to contact them. You should also take the telephone number of your car rental office or an associated breakdown business, since they will be able to help in case of difficulty. If you do have a breakdown, try to take your vehicle off the highway while waiting for assistance.

E

ELECTRICITY *(corriente eléctrica)*

Mexico uses the 120V/60Hz system, the same as the US and Canada. Travelers from other countries will need an adapter for their appliances – buy one at home or at the airport rather than waiting until you arrive.

EMBASSIES AND CONSULATES *(embajadas y consulados)*

There are consulates in Cancún for the following countries:
Canada: Consular Agency, Centro Empresarial, Oficina E7, Blvd Kukulcán, km 12, Zona Hotelera (Hotel Zone), 77599 Cancún, Quintana Roo, tel: (998) 883-3360, www.canadainternational.gc.ca.
US: Consular Agency, Torre la Europea, Office 301, Blvd Kukulcán, km 13, Zona Hotelera (Hotel Zone), 77500 Cancún, Quintana Roo, tel: (998) 883-0272, https://mx.usembassy.gov.
UK: British Consulate General, Torre la Europea Office 202, Blvd Kukulcán km 12.5, Zona Hotelera (Hotel Zone), 77500 Cancún, Quintana Roo, 24-hour helpline: +52-55-1670-3200, www.gov.uk/government/world/organisations.

The embassies of Australia, Ireland, New Zealand and South Africa are in Mexico City.
Australia: Ruben Dario 55, Colonia Polanco, 11580, Mexico DF, tel: +52 (55) 1101-2200, http://mexico.embassy.gov.au.

Ireland: Blvd Avila Camacho 76-3, Colonia Lomas de Chapultepec, 11000, Mexico DF, tel: +52 (55) 5522-5803, www.dfa.ie/irish-embassy/mexico.

New Zealand: Avenida Jaime Balmes No 8, 4th Floor, Colonia Los Morales, Polanco, 11510, Mexico DF, tel: +52 (55) 5283-9460, www.mfat.govt.nz/en/countries-and-regions.

South Africa: Andres Bello 10, Forum Building, 9th Floor, Colonia Polanco, 11560 Mexico DF, tel: +521 (55) 1100-4970, www.dirco.gov.za/foreign/sa_abroad/sam.htm.

EMERGENCIES (emergencias) (See also Police)

The emergency telephone number (similar to 911 in the US or 999 in the UK) is 066 or 911, but there are also separate telephone numbers for each emergency service in each town. It would help to have a Spanish speaker with you when you make the call; otherwise enlist the help of your hotel receptionist or tourist information office.

Police (policía): Cancún tel: 998/884-1913; Cozumel tel: 987/872-0409.

G

GAY AND LESBIAN TRAVELERS

Mexico is a conservative country with a deep Catholic faith. Because of this, overt displays of affection between the same sex are not seen within society and would be regarded as shocking. However, there is no undercurrent of harassment within society and gay individuals should have no concerns about visiting the Yucatán.

GETTING THERE

By air to Cancún. The following airlines fly to Cancún from the US: United Airlines www.united.com; American Airlines www.aa.com; Frontier Airlines www.flyfrontier.com; Delta Air Lines www.delta.com; Southwest Airlines www.southwest.com; JetBlue www.jetblue.com; Virgin America www.virginamerica.com; Spirit Airlines www.southwest.com; Alaska Airlines www.alaskaair.com (seasonal).

Package plans (flights/hotels/meals for one price) are available from any number of companies and can offer big savings compared to making separate arrangements for each element of your vacation. The websites www.signaturetravelnetwork.com, www.expedia.com, www.travelyucatan.com, www.travelocity.com are just a few places where you can start looking.

Direct, non-stop flights from the UK are operated by British Airways www.britishairways.com, Thomas Cook Airlines www.thomascookair lines.com, Thomson Airways www.thomson.co.uk and Virgin Atlantic www.virginatlantic.com. From South Africa and Australia/New Zealand, you will find the most sensible connections would be through a US airport with onward flight to Cancún.

By Boat. Those who fly to Cancún and do not wish to connect to Cozumel by plane must take the land route to Playa del Carmen and transfer by ferry. This 40–50 minute trip leaves every hour from 5am–11pm (the Playa del Carmen to Cozumel route). The bus service from Cancún to the passenger jetty in Playa del Carmen is regular, reliable, and inexpensive. The main bus station in Cancún is on Avenida Tulum.

A number of cruise lines make stops at Cozumel, with trips to the surrounding Maya sites. Puerto Calica, just south of Playa del Carmen, is another port of call, and Progreso is a popular alternative for people wanting to visit Mérida and the great Maya sites of Chichén Itzá and Uxmal. The main departure points are Miami and Puerto Rico.

GUIDES AND TOURS *(guías; visitas guidas)*

All the major archaeological sites usually have English-speaking guides waiting at the entrance to offer their services.

There are a number of commercial companies organizing morning or day tours to sites around Cancún and Cozumel. Tours may include lunch and a guide and offer a chance to swim or snorkel in addition to seeing the temples. From Isla Mujeres you can take tours with a number of operators to Isla Contoy for a day of snorkeling. There are also birdwatching tours of the coastal mangrove lagoons at Celestún and Río Lagartos. At Celestún, contact the Cultur visitors' center for birdwatching tours; at Río Lagartos Río Lagartos Adventures www.riolagartosnaturetours.com, which offers flamingo-, crocodile- and birdwatching tours. Hacienda Chichén www.haciendachichen.com has birdwatching guided tours. Iluminado Tours www.casakin.org in Mérida provides multi-day tours of the Mayan ruins and towns. And for tours of the Sian Ka'an Biosphere Reserve, visit the offices of the reserve located in the town of Tulum www.visitsiankaan.com.

> We'd like an English-speaking guide. **Queremos un guía que hable inglés.**
> I need an English interpreter. **Necesito un intérprete de inglés.**

H

HEALTH AND MEDICAL CARE

There are no immediate health concerns to worry about before your trip to the Yucatán. Always take out adequate insurance to cover emergency health problems, repatriation, or hospital treatment.

You will not need any inoculations unless you have traveled from a risk area to reach Mexico. However, if you intend to tour farther south into Belize or Guatemala, you should take advice from your doctor. Mosquitoes are a problem. Always carry insect repellent and apply it regularly when you visit the archaeological sites, and after dark no matter where you are.

There are numerous English-speaking doctors and medical facilities in Cancún, Cozumel, along the Riviera Maya and in Mérida, so if there is a problem you should have no difficulty finding help. Your hotel will always have the services of an English-speaking doctor on hand. There are good hospitals in Cancún (Hospital Americano, tel: 998/884-6133) and in Mérida (Centro Médico de la Americas, tel: 999/926-2111). You should have no problem obtaining most over-the-counter drugs – you'll find pharmacies in large supermarkets and town centers. By law, pharmacies take turns being open for 24 hours a day.

The risk of stomach upsets is nowhere near as great as it used to be. Times have moved on and the water you are served at a restaurant or the ice that goes in your juice or *licuado* is all *agua purificada* (purified water), and thus perfectly safe. Salads are prepared using *agua purificada*, so they, too, are safe. This applies not just to Cancún, but all towns with a restaurant trade. There may be the odd exception that proves the rule, and you shouldn't push your luck with roadside juice sellers, for example, but the days of 'Montezuma's revenge' are almost gone. If you do become ill, take plenty of fluids with a little salt and sugar to avoid dehydration, try some Pepto Bismol, and contact a doctor if those things don't do the trick.

The sun of the Yucatán is hot and strong, and in Cancún the sand reflects a great deal of heat and light. Always limit your time in the sun for the first few days to avoid sunburn, and apply a sun protection product regularly. Carry a covering layer (a long-sleeved shirt perhaps) that you can put on if you can't find any shade. Always wear a hat and sunglasses to avoid damage to the eyes. Be particularly careful with children's skin – always keep it protected with clothing or a sunblock product.

L

LANGUAGE

The official language of Mexico is Spanish, though a slightly different dialect than that spoken in Spain. Some 10 percent of the population speak an indigenous Indian language, and you will find that in the countryside of the Yucatán many people will speak the native Maya language.

English is understood and spoken by the vast majority of people in the tourist areas, though they will still undoubtedly welcome any attempts by visitors to speak Spanish. You will find some basic Latin-American Spanish phrases throughout this book, but for more comprehensive help, the *Berlitz Latin-American Spanish for Travelers* phrase book covers most situations you are likely to encounter.

M

MAPS

If you intend to stay around the Hotel Zone in Cancún, or on Cozumel or Mujeres, you will find maps at the local tourist offices. For touring out of the resort areas, you will need more detailed information. AAA produces comprehensive maps of the Yucatán region. Good maps of Mérida and the Yucatán Peninsula can be found on www.mapquest.com and www.yucatantoday.com.

MEDIA

The News is Mexico's English-language daily. Published in Mexico City, it can be found at major newsstands in the region (www.thenews.mx). Major US newspapers can be purchased in all the resort areas, along with some European papers in Playa de Carmen, though these are generally a day old.

Most large hotels will have satellite or cable TV with major US channels such as CNNand ESPN. And almost every town or major hotel now has an internet café or internet access.

MONEY *(moneda)*

Currency. The unit of currency in Mexico is the peso, denoted by a $ sign. US dollars are accepted at most businesses along the coast, but not in the inland areas. To avoid confusion between the US$ and the peso, most stores and restaurants in the tourist areas will quote US dollar prices with the abbreviation 'Dlls' or 'USD.' When buying goods in markets always make sure that you know whether you are negotiating in US dollars or Mexican pesos.

Peso notes are printed in the following denominations: $20, 50, 100, 200, 500 and 1000. Coins are $1, 2, 5, 10 and 20. Each peso is split into 100 *centavos*, though these are not generally found in cities or tourist resorts. However, if you travel to country markets and small settlements, these smaller coins are still in circulation; you will find them in denominations of 5, 10, 20, and 50c. Small change is always in short supply in Mexico, so keep any you come across.

Currency exchange. Currency can be exchanged at a number of places, with the best rates available at banks. Opening hours have expanded to about 9am–5pm Monday–Friday and 9am–noon on Saturdays, though you may not find them open when you expect to. The commercial tourist exchange houses *(casas de cambio)* are open longer hours than banks but may offer a less advantageous rate. Airports also have currency exchange kiosks, but these offer the lowest rates.

Credit cards *(tarjetas de crédito)*. Credit cards are widely accepted in shops, restaurants, and at attractions in the main resorts. Outside these areas always ask whether they are accepted. Gas stations only deal in cash.

ATMs. The easiest (and least costly) way of obtaining local currency is by using an ATM machine with your debit/credit card. Any major bank such as Banamex, found in most towns, will have an ATM inside; machines are also strategically located in Cancún's shopping plazas. Some machines in Cancún and Cozumel issue pesos and US dollars.

Travelers' checks *(cheque de viajero)*. Travelers' checks can be cashed at banks and exchange kiosks (take your passport as ID), though there will be a charge for the service and it's becoming increasingly difficult to cash them.

I want to change some dollars/pounds. **Quiero cambiar dólares/libras.**

Do you accept travelers' checks? **¿Acepta usted cheques de viajero?**

Can I pay with this credit card? **¿Puedo pagar con esta tarjeta de crédito?**

How much does it cost? **¿Cuánto es?**

Do you have anything less expensive? **¿Tiene algo más barato?**

O

OPEN HOURS

Archaeological sites are generally open daily from 8am–5pm, though some are open shorter hours on Sundays. Government offices are open from 9am–5pm, probably longer if they deal with visitors, and though the siesta has disappeared in the resort area, you may still find the person you need to speak to is absent from 2pm–4pm. They will make up their hours by working later into the evening.

Stores in tourist areas are generally open until 9pm. Car rental and tour operator offices open at 9am and close between 7pm and 9pm.

P

POLICE *(policía)*

The police have a checkered reputation throughout Mexico, but their image is more positive in the tourist areas of the Yucatán. Police wear brown and beige uniforms; you can find them patrolling the Hotel Zone and downtown in Cancún, Cozumel and central Mérida. The main police station in Cancún is on Avenida Tulum, next to the tourist office. In the Hotel Zone there is a 'tourist police' station in Boulevard Kukulcán, km 13, opposite Torre La Europea. Mérida also has a 'tourist police' force patrolling the downtown area. They speak English and wear light beige pants in contrast to the brown pants of the normal police force.

If you need to report a theft or crime and your Spanish isn't strong, try to have a Spanish speaker with you. The emergency number to call for the police is 066 or 911.

> I've lost my wallet/purse/passport. **He perdido mi cartera/ bolsa/pasaporte.**

POST OFFICES *(correos)*

The main post office in Cancún is on Avenida Sunyaxchén/Xel-Ha; open Monday–Friday 8am–6pm, Saturday 9am–1pm. In Cozumel, the main post office is Avenida Melgar a few minutes south of the pier; open Monday–Friday 9am–1pm and 3pm–6pm, Saturday 9am–1pm.

Stamps *(estampillas, timbres)* can be bought at newsagents or drugstores. When you buy your postcards ask if you can buy stamps at the same time. Mailboxes are red. Most hotels will post cards for you, so ask at reception. The postal service is very slow, often 14 days to North America and longer to Europe. If you have anything that is urgent or valuable, it would be better to send it by commercial carrier.

PUBLIC HOLIDAYS *(dias festivos)*

National holidays fall on the following dates.

January 1 *Año Nuevo* (New Year's Day)
February 5 *Aniversario de la Constitución* (Constitution Day)
March 21 *Nacimiento de Benito Juárez* (Juárez's birthday)
Variable *Pascua, Semana Santa* (Easter, Holy Week)
May 1 *Día del Trabajo* (Labor Day)
May 5 *Batalla de Puebla* (Anniversary of the Battle of Puebla)
September 1 *Informe presidencial* (First Day of Congress)
September 16 *Día de la Independencia* (Independence Day)
October 12 *Día de la Raza* (Columbus Day/Day of the Race)
November 2 *Día de los Muertos* (Day of the Dead)
November 20 *Aniversario de la Revolucion* (Anniversary of the Revolution)
December 12 *Día de Nuestra Señora de Guadalupe* (Day of Our Lady of Guadalupe)
December 25 *Navidad* (Christmas Day)

PUBLIC TRANSPORTATION *(transporte publico)*

Buses. In Cancún, a regular bus service runs through the Hotel Zone to downtown and back for $8.50. Long-distance buses that run down the coast to Playa del Carmen and Tulum, or west to Mérida, depart from the bus station on Avenida Tulum at Avenida Uxmal. Prices are very inexpensive: the fare with the Riviera bus company from Cancún to Playa del Carmen is around $60.

Taxis. Taxis are numerous along the Zona Turística in Cancún – they are green-and-white and will sound their horn as they drive past. You can hail them on the street, or your hotel will call one for you. Fares for each journey are pre-set – ask your hotel reception or tourist information office how much it should be. In Cozumel taxis can be found outside the main pier – where a list of fares is posted – and at the cruise ports. In Mérida, taxis can be found at Parque Santa Anna or next to the Jose Peón Contreras Theatre on Calle 60. Taxis can also be hired by the morning or day for sightseeing. Always agree on a price before setting out. If you are in a group of several people, it may be less expensive to take a taxi for the day than to book bus tours.

What is the fare for...? **Cuál es la tarifa a...?**

Ferries. Frequent ferry services run from Puerto Juárez (10 minutes from downtown Cancún) to Isla Mujeres. There are crossings every half hour, with the last one leaving Mujeres at 7.30pm. Less frequent and more expensive services run from Playa Linda Marine Terminal and Playa Caracol to Mujeres, but these may not run out of season.

Ferries to Cozumel from the mainland run from Playa del Carmen, with numerous crossings per day, the last one leaving at 10pm. A car ferry service is also available from Punta Venado, 5km (3 miles) south of Playa del Carmen.

R

RELIGION

Mexico is a predominantly Roman Catholic country and the population still worships regularly. Always dress conservatively when entering a Catholic place of worship.

T

TELEPHONE *(teléfonos)*

The international dialing code for Mexico is 52, preceded by 011 if calling from the US or Canada; 00 if calling from the UK. Almost all area codes are 3-digit (yet Mexico City metropolitan area's code is 55), followed by a 7-digit number. If dialing within the area, there is no need to dial the code.

The easiest way of calling locally or internationally is to use a Telmex phonecard, available for $30, $50 and $100 at most groceries and newsagents and usable at the ubiquitous Ladatel payphones. Most large hotels will have direct-dial facilities for local and international calls, but this is always more expensive than using a phonecard or credit cards.

International dialing codes are as follows (always prefix these codes with 00): US and Canada 1; UK 44; Australia 61; New Zealand 64; South Africa 27; Ireland 353.

TIME ZONES

The state of Quintana Roo (Cancún, Cozumel) is in the same time zone as US Eastern Standard Time, 5 hrs behind GMT, but does not change to daylight saving in summer.

The state of Yucatán (Mérida) is in the same time zone as US Central Standard Time, 6 hrs behind GMT and changes to daylight saving in summer.

Cancún	Mérida	New York	London	Johannesburg	Sydney
noon	11am	noon	5pm	7pm	4am

TIPPING *(propina; servicio)*

Service charges are not generally included in the final check in hotels and restaurants and, because wages are low in Mexico, service personnel rely on money earned in tips. Ten to 20 percent is standard in restaurants, $10-30 per bag for bellboys, $30-50 per day for hotel maids. And try to tip in pesos whenever possible.

TOILETS

Clean and well-maintained public restrooms can be found at shopping malls, most archaeological sites and most Pemex stations. If there is an attendant, expect to pay a small fee. Men's rooms will be labeled *caballeros*, *hombres*, or 'H'; women's *damas*, *mujeres*, or 'M.'

> Where are the restrooms... **Dondé están los sanitarios?**

TOURIST INFORMATION *(oficinas de información turística)*

The following are the addresses of overseas Mexico Tourism Board's offices.

Canada: 1 Place Ville Marie, Suite 1931, Montréal, Québec H3B 2C3, tel: (514) 871-1052; 2 Bloor Street West, Suite 1502, Toronto, Ontario M4W 3E2, tel: (416) 925-0078; De Granville Street, Suite 658-409, Vancouver, British Columbia V6C 1T2, tel: (604) 669-2845.

US: 152 Madison Avenue, suite 1800, New York, NY 10016, tel: (212) 308-2110; 225 North Michigan Avenue, suite 1800, Chicago, IL 60601, tel: (312) 228-0513; 2401 West 6th Street, 5th Floor, Los Angeles, CA 90057, tel: (213) 739-6336; 4507 San Jacinto, suite 308, Houston, TX 77004, tel: (713) 772-2581; 1399 SW 1st Avenue, Miami, FL 33130, tel: (786) 621-2909

UK: Wakefield House, 41 Trinity Square, London EC3N 4DJ, tel: (020) 7488-9392

There are two state tourist offices covering the locations in this guide: **Quintana Roo**: Calzada del Centenario #622, 77019 Chetumal, tel: (983) 8352-0860; **Yucatán**: Calle 59a #242, 79000 Mérida, tel: (999) 925-5186. Tourist information can be found locally at **Cancún** (Avenida Náder/Cobá, Downtown Cancún, tel: 998/887-3379), **Cozumel** (Plaza del Sol, Avenida Benito Juárez, tel: 987/872-0972), and **Mérida** (Calle 60 below the Péon Contreras Theatre, tel: 999/924-9290; also in the Governor's Palace).

There are a wide variety of information magazines and brochures available, including the informative *Yucatán Today* for Mérida, and *Cancún Tips* available all over Cancún. Playa del Carmen, Tulum, Akumal and other resorts also have their own information magazines.

W

WEBSITES

The following may be useful before you make your trip:

www.cancun.travel has useful information about Cancún.

www.travelyucatan.com is a comprehensive travel guide to Cancún and the entire peninsula which also provides booking services.

www.yucatanliving.com is an insider's guide to Mérida and the Yucatán Peninsula.

www.yucatantoday.com is a tourist guide for the Yucatán.

www.rivieramaya.com is run by the Riviera Maya Tourism promotion board and is a good source of information for the entire area.

www.akumalbayinfo.com is full of useful information about Akumal

www.locogringo.com provides lodging and other information for the entire Riviera Maya.

RECOMMENDED HOTELS

The Hotel Zone of Cancún is a modern resort – all the hotels were built after 1970, therefore they are very much alike in terms of amenities and standards. All have air-conditioning, swimming pools, restaurants and beach access. There are no budget accommodations, but standards rise to luxury, and there are thousands of beds here, with large and small hotels to choose from. Downtown Cancún has more moderate and budget hotels, though it is a short bus ride to the beach. Cozumel and Isla Mujeres both have a range of accommodations from luxury to basic, as does the resort of Playa del Carmen. Mérida, too, has hotels in every price bracket.

The following list covers a range of hotels in all price brackets (price is for a double room in high season; prices in the resorts can be 50 percent lower Apr–Dec).

$$$$$	above US$350
$$$$	US$200–350
$$$	US$120–200
$$	US$75–120
$	below US$75

CANCÚN

Downtown

Adhara Hacienda Cancún $$$ *Avenida Nader 1 S.M. 2, tel: (998) 881-6500,* www.adharacancun.com. Occupying a building inspired by hacienda architecture, the Adhara Hacienda has a total of 174 rooms. Outdoor pool. Mexican and international specialties served at Alehna Restaurant.

Eco-Hotel El Rey del Caribe $–$$ *Avenida Uxmal and Avenida Nader, tel: (998) 884-2028,* www.ecohotelreydelcaribe.com. Environmentally-friendly hotel. Simply-furnished rooms with kitchenettes open to a central garden area with a pool. Spa services available. 31 rooms.

Hotel HC Internacional $ *Avenida Uxmal No. 44, tel: (998) 884-0550,* http://hotelhcinternacional.com-cancun.com. Long established hotel with reasonable rates and amenities. Rooms include cable TV, air conditioning and free Wi-Fi. Just 100m from the bus station. 28 rooms.

Hotel Margaritas $ *Avenida Yaxchilan 41, SM 22, tel: (998) 881-6523,* www. hotelmargaritascancun.com.mx. Inexpensive hotel with 74 rooms, each with air conditioning, television and free Wi-Fi. Restaurant and bar.

Hotel Plaza Kokai $ *Avenida Uxmal No. 26, SM 2-A, tel: (998) 193-3180,* www.hotel-plaza-kokai-cancun.com. Small business hotel, one block east of Avenida Tulum. Clean, air-conditioned rooms with marble bathrooms and small first floor swimming pool. Restaurant and bar, free Wi-Fi. 44 rooms, two junior suites and one penthouse.

Pueblito Hostel $ *Calle Alcatraces 50, SM 22,* www.hostelworld.com. Co-ed hostel a block from Palapas Park. Single rooms and dorms with shared baths. Free breakfast and Wi-Fi. Open 24 hours.

Hotel Zone

Le Blanc Spa Resort $$$$$ *Boulevard Kukulcán km 10, tel: 1-866-599-6674,* www.leblancsparesort.com. Chic minimalist hotel with 260 air conditioned luxurious rooms with balconies. World-class spa.

Fiesta Americana Condesa Cancún $$$$$ *Boulevard Kukulcán km 16.5, tel: (998) 881-4200,* www.fiestaamericana.com.mx. Beautiful hotel with warm atmosphere and world-class quality and service. Architecture hints of traditional Mexico. Large pool area leads down to a white sandy beach. Four restaurants and a full-service spa. 476 rooms and 26 suites with all modern amenities.

Iberostar Cancún $$$$$ *Boulevard Kukulcán km 17, tel: (998) 881-8000,* www.iberostar.com. Completely renovated in 2011, this luxurious hotel features five restaurants, spa, state-of-the-art fitness center, seven pools and one of the widest beaches in Cancún. The hotel also has its own 18-hole golf course, tennis courts and a kids club. 426 rooms.

NIZUC Resort and Spa $$$$$ *Boulevard Kukulcán km 21, tel: (998) 891-5700*, www.nizuc.com. This new luxury resort is located in Punta Nizuc. It boasts cutting-edge architecture, two beaches, a spa by ESPA and six gourmet restaurants. 274 suites and villas.

Paradisus Cancún $$$$$ *Boulevard Kukulcán km 16.5, tel: (998) 881-1100*, www.melia.com. Beautiful hotel shaped like five pyramids with glass roofs. The man-made waterfalls and fountains and the cascading plants in the huge main interior atrium give the feeling of a Yucatecan *cenote*. Four pools, nine restaurants, stores, a golf course. 668 rooms.

Park Royal Cancún $$$$$ *Boulevard Kukulcán, km 12.5, tel: 1-888-774-0040*, www.parkroyalcancunresort.com. A sleek hotel in two pyramid-shaped towers just steps away from La Isla Shopping Center. Rooms have views of the lagoon or the sea. Three swimming pools. 288 rooms.

Secrets the Vine Cancún $$$$$ *Boulevard Kukulcán, km 14.5, tel: (998) 848-9400*, www.secretsresorts.com. Adults-only chic resort with a swimming pool, fitness center, six gourmet restaurants and a 24 hours-operating cafe. 497 rooms and suites.

ISLA MUJERES

Bucaneros Hotel & Suites $–$$ *Avenida Hidalgo No. 11, tel: (998) 877-1228*, www.bucaneros.com. Family-run hotel and restaurant located just a short walk away from the turquoise water of the Playa Norte. Nice Mayan-Caribbean styled rooms. Air-conditioning, ceiling fan, and cable TV standard in the rooms. 20 rooms.

La Casa de los Sueños $$$$$ *Carretera Garrafón, tel: (998) 888-0370*, www.casasuenos.com. This beautiful building in the south of the island is an adults-only upscale b&b, serving continental breakfast and catering to the discerning traveler. Rooms are individually designed with high quality in mind. Swimming pool and meditation area, restaurant serving Asian Mexican fusion cuisine, 10 rooms. Excellent accompanying spa.

Suites Los Arcos $ *Avenida Hidalgo Colonial Centro, contact through Lost Oasis at tel: (998) 877-0951*, www.lostoasis.net. The comfortable suites in the centre of downtown Isla Mujeres are just a few blocks from Playa Norte; each has a kitchenette, cable TV, air conditioning and a balcony. Friendly, bilingual staff. Internet access is available. 12 rooms.

Hotel Na Balam $$$$ *Calle Zazil-Há No. 118, tel: (998) 881-4770*, www.nabalam.com. Located on Playa Norte, this boutique hotel has both poolside and beachfront rooms, each with terrace or balcony. Swimming pool and spa on site; yoga classes available. Oceanus Beach Club and Restaurant offers excellent dinners and drinks. 33 rooms.

Hotel Playa La Media Luna $$$ *Punta Norte, tel: (998) 877-0759*, www.playamedialuna.com. Located on Half Moon Beach in the northeast of the island, a two-minute walk from Playa Norte. Nicely appointed air conditioned rooms with TVs and ceiling fans, each with its own private balcony overlooking the beach; pool. 18 rooms.

Zoetry Villa Rolandi Isla Mujeres Cancún $$$$$ *Carretera Sac Bajo, Laguna Mar, tel: (998) 999-2000*, www.zoetryresorts.com. Exclusive Mexican-Mediterranean style hotel on the west coast of the island, complete with stone floors and tiled ceilings. All suites have an ocean view, marble bathrooms and full amenities. Onsite spa. Two restaurants: Casa Rolandi (Swiss-Northern Italian fare) and Le Métissage (French-Mexican fusion cuisine). 35 suites.

COZUMEL

Amaranto B&B $ *Calle 5 Sur between Ave 15 and Ave 20, tel: (987) 872-3219*, www.amarantobedandbreakfast.com. Comfortable, air-conditioned rooms with kitchenettes. Picnic and barbecue area. Wi-Fi in each room. Three bungalows and two apartments. Breakfast extra.

El Cid La Ceiba Beach Hotel $$$$ *Carretera Chankanaab, km 4.5, tel: 1-888-733-7308*, www.elcid.com. Lovely oceanfront resort. All rooms and suites feature kitchenettes, balconies and TVs. Two restaurants, bar and massage center available. 60 rooms.

Fiesta Americana Cozumel $$$$ *Carretera Chankanaab, km 7.5, tel: (987) 872-9600*, www.fiestamericana.com. Completely renovated in 2014, this beachfront resort faces the Palancar Reef and is located only minutes from restaurants, shopping and nightlife. Caters to divers. Pool, spa, six restaurants and several bars. 102 rooms.

Hacienda San Miguel $$ *Calle 10 Norte No. 500, between 5th Avenue and the Rafael Melgar, tel: (987) 872-1986*, www.haciendasanmiguel.com. Classic colonial-style hacienda hotel in downtown San Miguel with beautifully decorated rooms surrounding lush gardens. Units range from small studios to large suites and include kitchenettes and cable TV. 11 rooms.

Hostelito $ *Avenida 10 at Avenida 2 North, tel: (987) 869-8157.* Basic backpackers hostel with discounts for groups. Dorms and private rooms. Open 24 hours with internet cafe and kitchen. Beds have lockers big enough for scuba gear. One block from the main pier. 26 beds.

Melia Cozumel Golf $$$$$ *Costera Norte, km 5.8, tel: 1-800-906-3542*, www.melia.com. All-inclusive beach resort 10 minutes north of San Miguel. Three restaurants, two pools, wellness center, watersports, daily activities, kids' club, nightly entertainment. 18-hole golf course. 140 rooms.

Playa Azul Golf Scuba Spa $$$$$ *Carretera San Juan, km 4, Zona Hotelera Norte, tel: (987) 869-5160*, www.playa-azul.com. Exclusive hotel located on the beautiful San Juan beach. All rooms and suites have a balcony with stunning ocean views. Swimming pool, two restaurants, two bars and a beach club; fishing and diving available; golf at the Cozumel Country Club. 50 rooms.

PLAYA DEL CARMEN

Hotel Colibri Beach $$ *1a Avenida Norte between calles 10 and 12, tel: (984) 803-1090*, www.hotelcolibribeach.com. Pleasant hotel right on the beach, with spacious rooms and peaceful atmosphere; beach restaurant. Offers a choice of large rooms and more traditional cabañas, all recently remodelled and decorated in rustic Mexican style. 28 rooms, one suite and five cabañas.

Gran Porto Resort and Spa $$$$$ *Constituyentes No. 1, Playa del Carmen, tel: (984) 873-4000,* www.playaresorts.com. Located on the beach, rooms are Mexican in architectural style with large bathrooms and comfortable beds. Two swimming pools, fitness center, spa, ten restaurants, bars and lounges. 287 rooms.

Hotel Lunata $$$ *Avenida 5 between calles 6 and 8, tel: (984) 873-0884,* www.lunata.com. Pleasant hotel right on 5th Avenue at the heart of Playa del Carmen, incorporating a mixture of hacienda- and pueblo-style architecture. Rooms are finished to a high standard and include all modern amenities. Pleasant garden at the rear and a rooftop terrace. 10 rooms.

Mosquito Beach $$$$ *Calle 8, tel: (984) 873-1245,* www.mosquitoblue. com. This adults-only hotel has beautifully appointed rooms with marble showers and mahogany beds. The Mosquito restaurant has an inventive menu with Italian twist. There is also an outdoor pool and a bar. 33 rooms.

La Tortuga Hotel and Spa $$$ *Avenida 10 corner of Calle 14, tel: (984) 873-1484,* www.hotellatortugaspa.com. Adults-only boutique hotel located just around the corner from 5th Avenue. There are spacious rooms and junior suites. Amenities include a restaurant, bar and swimming pool, with associated spa next door. 51 rooms.

MÉRIDA

Casa del Balam $$$ *Calle 60, corner Calle 57, tel: (999) 924-8844,* www. casadelbalam.com. First-class hotel in the heart of Mérida, with beautiful patio gardens. Rooms are elegantly decorated with colonial antiques, wrought iron accessories and marble floors. Restaurant, bar and swimming pool. 51 rooms.

Luz en Yucatán $-$$ *Calle 55 No. 499 between calles 58 and 60, tel: (999) 924-0035,* www.luzenyucatan.com. Townhouse in the heart of Mérida with tastefully and individually furnished rooms and apartments, and enticing pool. Kitchenette and cable TV in every room.

Hotel MedioMundo $$–$$$ *Calle 55 No. 533 between calles 64 and 66;* *tel: (999) 924-5472,* www.hotelmediomundo.com. Family-operated hotel in a renovated 19th-century mansion. Rooms, each tastefully designed with its own individual features, are ranged around a tranquil, exotically-planted courtyard, and there is a terrace and pool at the back. 10 rooms.

La Misión de Fray Diego $$$ *Calle 61 between calles 64 and 66, tel: (999)* *924-1111,* www.lamisiondefraydiego.com. Fine little hotel in a restored 17th-century residence one block from the historic center, with elegant rooms and wonderful grounds. 20 standard rooms, four special category rooms, and two suites with Jacuzzi.

Hacienda Xcanatun $$$$ *Carretera Mérida–Progreso, km 12, tel: (999)* *941-0213,* www.xcanatun.com. A privately-owned small luxury hotel in a restored 18th-century hacienda just north of Mérida. The hotel has a beautifully designed interior, the rooms have all modern amenities, and the cuisine (international and Yucatecan) at the 'Casa de Piedra' restaurant is superb. 18 suites.

UXMAL

The Lodge at Uxmal $$$ *(opposite the site entrance), tel: (998) 887-2495,* www.mayaland.com. Pretty hotel blending Maya and European architectural styles, with *palapa* roofs, hacienda-style verandas and locally produced wood furnishings in the rooms. Two pools; open-air restaurant. 40 rooms.

Uxmal Resort Maya $$ *Carretera Merida-Campeche, km 78, tel: (997)* *930-0390,* www.uxmalresortmaya.com. Hotel with views of the ruins at Uxmal, though it is 3km (2 miles) from the site entrance. Large rooms with basic but clean with balconies; pool; restaurant. 82 rooms.

CHICHÉN ITZÁ

Hacienda Chichén $$$ *Zona Hotelera behind the archeological site of* *Chichén Itzá, tel: (999) 920-8407,* www.haciendachichen.com. Just behind the Mayan ruins, the Hacienda has individual cottages uniquely decorated in Mexican styles. Restaurant and bar, high speed internet, large pool, spa. 28 rooms. Hotel subscribes to sustainable tourism practices.

Mayaland Resort $$$ *Carretera Mérida-Cancún, km 120, tel: (998) 887-2495*, www.mayaland.com. Offers hotel rooms in the main building and terraced cottages in lush tropical surroundings. Cottages have thatched *palapa*-style roofs and hammocks on the terraces. Three pools; several restaurants; shuttle to the site. 95 rooms.

AKUMAL

Grand Oasis Tulum $$$$$ *Cancún-Chetumal Carretera km 252, tel: (984) 848-7500*, www.oasishotels.com. Magnificent all-inclusive tropical resort near Akumal Beach. Nine restaurants, nightly entertainment. 228 rooms.

TULUM

Hemingway Romantic Resort $$$ *Boca Paila Road, tel: (984) 114-2321*, www.hemingwaytulum.net. Romantic cabañas in garden or beach settings. Breakfast served in the seaside restaurant included. The restaurant serving Mediterranean food is open for dinner every day until 10pm. Personalized yoga classes. 14 cabañas and nine bungalows.

Maya Tulum $$$ *Boca Paila Road, tel: (984) 116-4495*, www.mayatulum. com. Luxury beachside, ocean or garden view cabañas. A favorite for yoga retreats; there is also a spa and a huge palapa-roofed restaurant serving vegetarian and seafood meals. 46 rooms.

Zamas $$$ *Boca Paila Road, tel: (984) 688-8591*, www.zamas.com. Beachside bungalows with ocean or garden views. Very popular restaurant and live music on weekends. 17 rooms.

INDEX

INSIGHT ⊙ GUIDES **POCKET GUIDE**

CANCÚN & COZUMEL

First Edition 2017

Editor: Frances Moloney
Author: Lindsay Bennett
Head of Production: Rebeka Davies
Picture Editor: Tom Smyth
Cartography Update: Carte
Update Production: Apa Digital
Photography Credits: Alamy 4ML, 31, 45; Alex
Havret/Apa Publications 6L, 6R, 7, 7R, 88, 92,
99, 101, 102, 105; AWL Images 1, 26, 80; Dagli
Orti/REX/Shutterstock 21; Daniel Schwen
57; de Spirse Taylor/REX/Shutterstock 5MC;
Eye
Im
85,
iSt
36
Pic
53
Co

Hong Kong, Taiwan and China:
Apa Publications (HK) Ltd;
hongkongoffice@insightguides.com
Worldwide: Apa Publications (UK) Ltd;
sales@insightguides.com

**Special Sales, Content Licensing
and CoPublishing**
Insight Guides can be purchased in bulk
quantities at discounted prices. We can
create special editions, personalised jackets
and corporate imprints tailored to your
needs. sales@insightguides.com;
www.insightguides.biz

All Rights Reserved
    (CH) AG and
    UK) Ltd
    y CTPS
    may be reproduced,
    system or transmitted in
    electronic, mechanical,
    ding or otherwise, without
    ssion from Apa Publications.

Di
U
(U
Ur
Pu
Au
in
So
si

en made to provide accurate
publication, but changes are
isher cannot be responsible
ss, inconvenience or injury.
te it if readers would call our
ors or outdated information.
our suggestions; please
@insightguides.com
.com